FOR ORGANS, PIANOS & ELECTRONIC KEYBOARDS

E-Z PLAY TODAY

405

the 20th Century Love Songs

ISBN 0-634-02208-3

HAL•LEONARD®
CORPORATION

7777 W. BLUEMOUND RD. P.O. BOX 13819 MILWAUKEE, WI 53213

E-Z Play® Today Music Notation © 1975 by HAL LEONARD CORPORATION
E-Z PLAY and EASY ELECTRONIC KEYBOARD MUSIC are registered trademarks of HAL LEONARD CORPORATION.

Visit Hal Leonard Online at
www.halleonard.com

CONTENTS

4 Almost Paradise
Ann Wilson & Mike Reno

10 Always
recorded by various artists, including
Patsy Cline
Billie Holiday
Frank Sinatra

7 Always in My Heart
(Siempre en mi corazón)
Glenn Miller

12 And I Love Her
The Beatles

14 And So It Goes
Billy Joel

18 Anytime You Need a Friend
Mariah Carey

22 Bésame Mucho (Kiss Me Much)
recorded by various artists, including
Jimmy Dorsey

24 Cherish
The Association

28 (They Long to Be) Close to You
The Carpenters

34 Do I Love You Because
You're Beautiful?
from the musical CINDERELLA

31 Ev'ry Time We Say Goodbye
recorded by various artists, including
Benny Goodman
Annie Lennox
Anita O'Day

36 Everytime You Go Away
Paul Young

39 Feelings
Morris Albert

42 The First Time Ever I Saw Your Face
Roberta Flack

48 Friends
Michael W. Smith

45 The Glory of Love
recorded by various artists, inclu
The Five Keys
Benny Goodman
Bette Midler

52 A Groovy Kind of Love
Phil Collins
The Mindbenders

60 Grow Old with Me
Mary Chapin Carpenter
John Lennon

62 Here, There and Everywhere
The Beatles

64 I Could Write a Book
from the musical PAL JOEY

66 I Left My Heart in San Francisco
Tony Bennett

55 I Will Be Here
Steven Curtis Chapman

68 I'll Be There
Mariah Carey
The Jackson 5

70 I've Grown Accustomed to Her Fa
from the musical MY FAIR LADY

76 If
Bread

78 In My Life
The Beatles

73 It's Impossible (Somos novios)
Perry Como
Luis Miguel

80 Just One More Chance
recorded by various artists, inclu
Bing Crosby
Dean Martin
Les Paul and Mary Ford

82 Just the Way You Are
Billy Joel

86 Make It with You
Bread

90 More Than You Know
recorded by various artists, including
  Gogi Grant
  Billie Holiday
  Barbra Streisand

96 My Cherie Amour
Stevie Wonder

93 My Foolish Heart
recorded by various artists, including
  Billy Eckstine
  Bill Evans

98 My Heart Stood Still
from the musical
A CONNECTICUT YANKEE

100 (You Make Me Feel Like)
A Natural Woman
Aretha Franklin
Carole King

104 The Nearness of You
recorded by various artists, including
  Dinah Shore
  Sarah Vaughan

106 Nobody Loves Me Like You Do
Anne Murray with Dave Loggins

110 Save the Best for Last
Vanessa Williams

116 Saving All My Love for You
Whitney Houston

120 September Song
from the musical
KNICKERBOCKER HOLIDAY

122 Something
The Beatles

124 Sometimes When We Touch
Dan Hill

128 Star Dust
recorded by various artists, including
  Louis Armstrong
  Artie Shaw

130 There's a Small Hotel
from the musical ON YOUR TOES

132 True Love
Bing Crosby & Grace Kelly

134 Unexpected Song
from the musical SONG AND DANCE

113 Valentine
Jim Brickman with Martina McBride

138 The Very Thought of You
recorded by various artists, including
  Benny Carter
  Billie Holiday
  Ray Noble

140 What'll I Do?
recorded by various artists, including
  Nat "King" Cole
  Linda Ronstadt
  Frank Sinatra

142 When I Fall in Love
recorded by various artists, including
  Nat "King" Cole
  Doris Day
  Celine Dion and Clive Griffin

144 Where or When
from the musical BABES IN ARMS

146 With a Song in My Heart
recorded by various artists, including
  Perry Como

148 Wonderful Tonight
Eric Clapton

154 You and I
Stevie Wonder

156 You Are the Sunshine of My Life
Stevie Wonder

151 You're Nearer
recorded by various artists, including
  Judy Garland
  Shirley Horn
  Steve Lawrence

158 You've Got a Friend
Carole King
James Taylor

Almost Paradise
Love Theme from the Paramount Motion Picture FOOTLOOSE

Registration 8
Rhythm: Rock or 8 Beat

Words by Dean Pitchford
Music by Eric Carmen

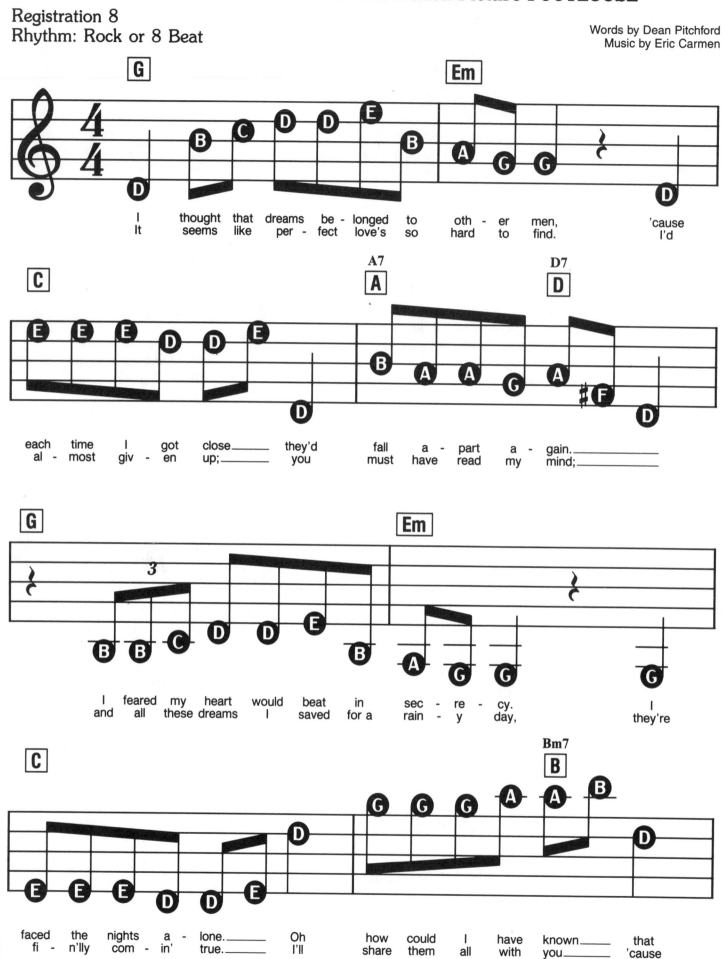

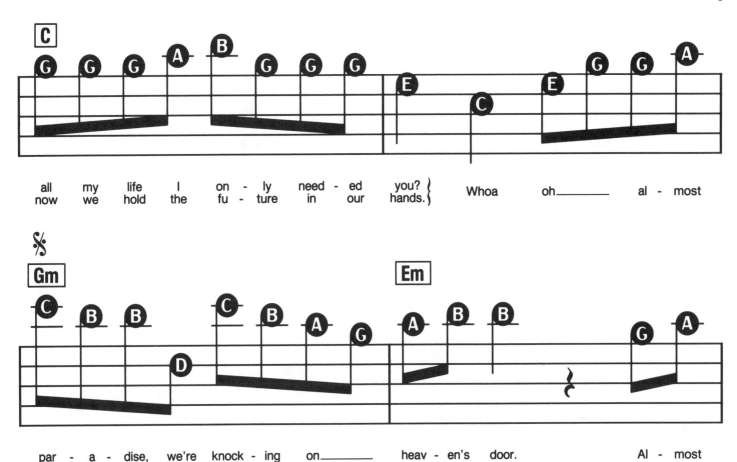

all my life I on - ly need - ed you? Whoa oh_____ al - most
now we hold the fu - ture in our hands.

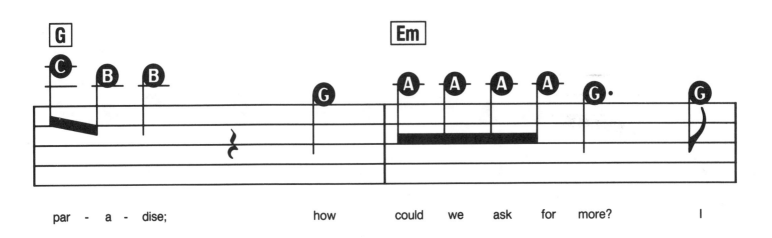

par - a - dise, we're knock - ing on_____ heav - en's door. Al - most

par - a - dise; how could we ask for more? I

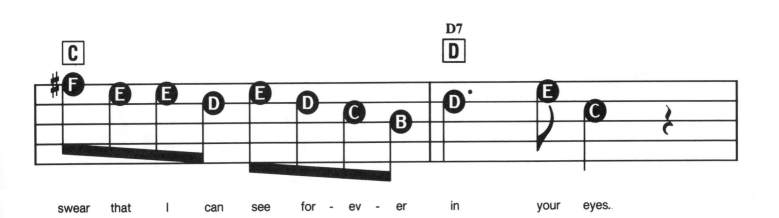

swear that I can see for - ev - er in your eyes.

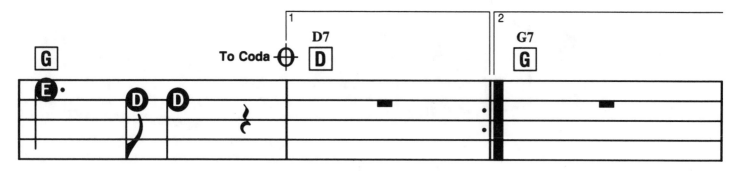

Par - a - dise.

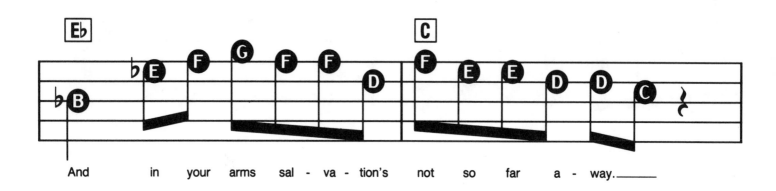

And in your arms sal - va - tion's not so far a - way.____

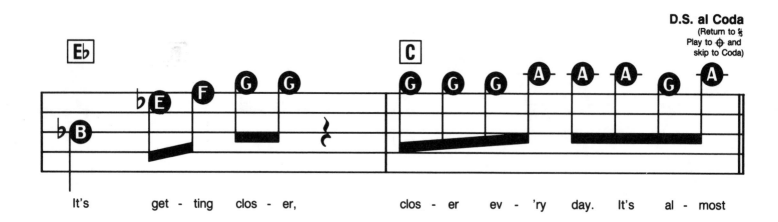

It's get - ting clos - er, clos - er ev - 'ry day. It's al - most

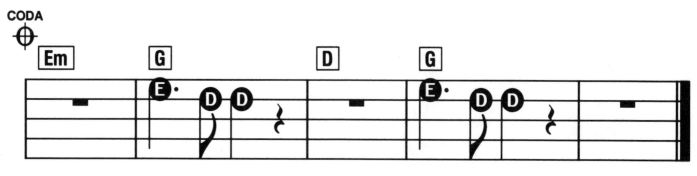

Par - a - dise, par - a - dise.

Always in My Heart
(Siempre en mi corazón)

Registration 4
Rhythm: Rhumba or Latin

Music and Spanish Words by
Ernesto Lecuona
English Words by Kim Gannon

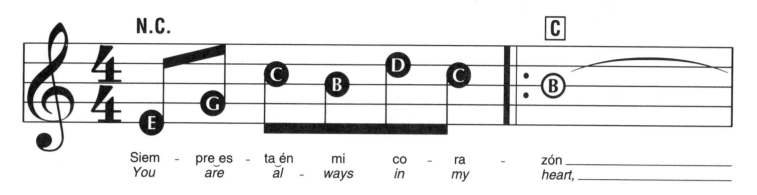

Siem - pre es - ta én mi co - ra - zón _____
You are al - ways in my heart, _____

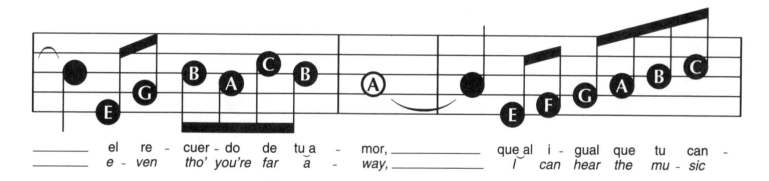

_____ el re - cuer - do de tu a - mor, _____ que al i - gual que tu can -
_____ *e - ven tho' you're far a - way,* _____ *I can hear the mu - sic*

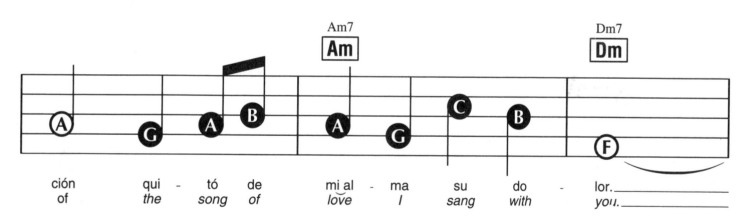

ción qui - tó de mi al - ma su do - lor. _____
of *the song of love I sang with you.* _____

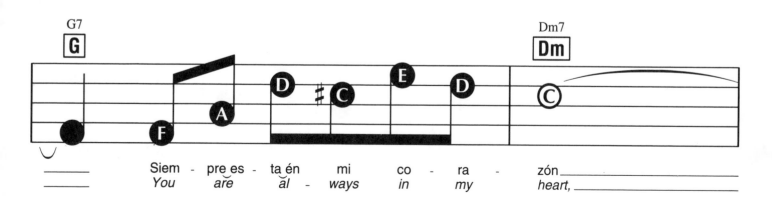

Siem - pre es - ta én mi co - ra - zón _____
You are al - ways in my heart, _____

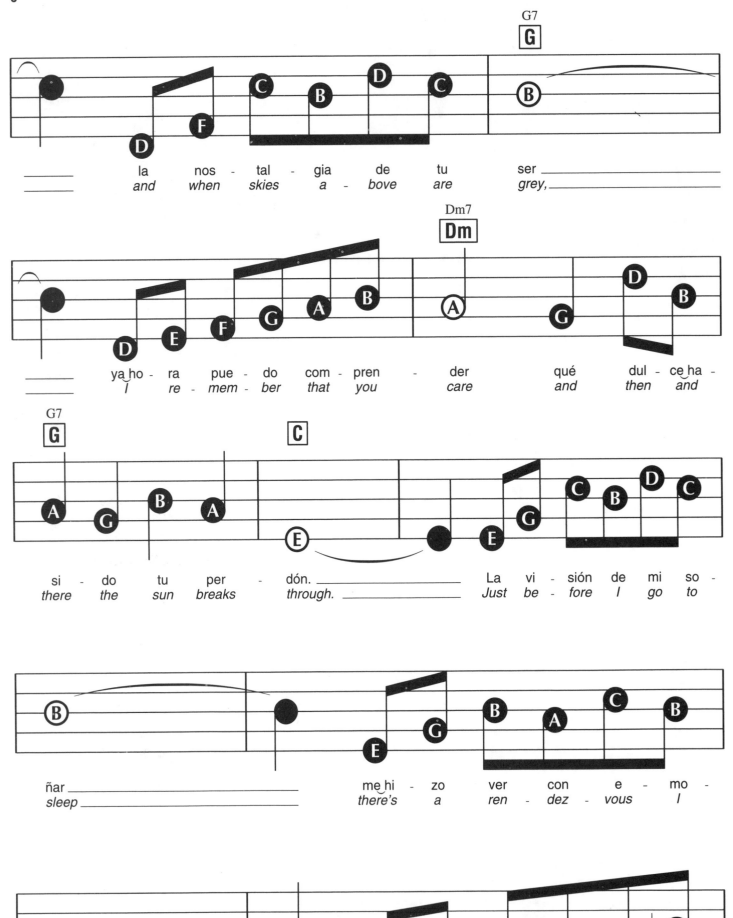

la nos - tal - gia de tu ser _____
and when skies a - bove are grey,

ya ho - ra pue - do com - pren - der qué dul - ce ha
I re - mem - ber that you care and then and

si - do tu per - dón. _____ La vi - sión de mi so -
there the sun breaks through. _____ Just be - fore I go to

ñar _____ me hi - zo ver con e - mo -
sleep _____ there's a ren - dez - vous I

ción, _____ que fue tu al - ma ins - pi - ra -
keep. _____ And the dream I al - ways

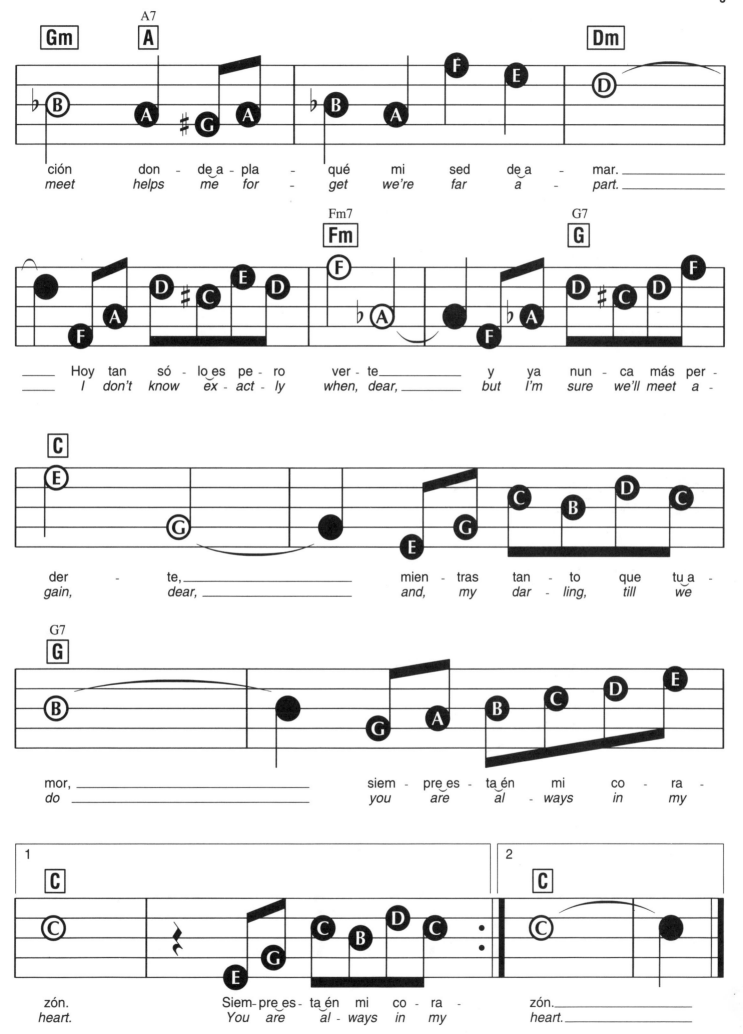

Always

Registration 2
Rhythm: Waltz

Words and Music by
Irving Berlin

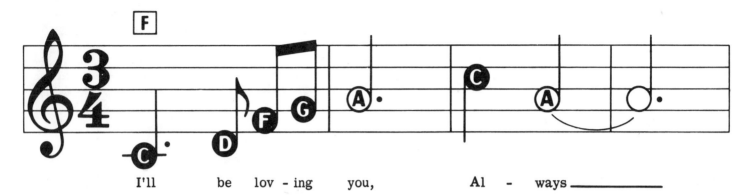

I'll be lov - ing you, Al - ways ____

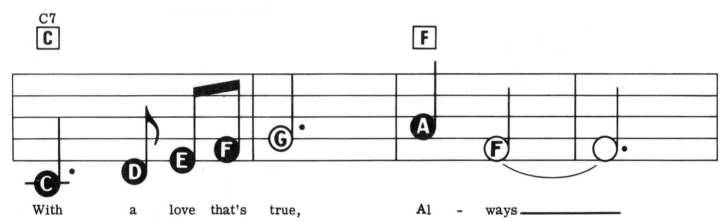

With a love that's true, Al - ways ____

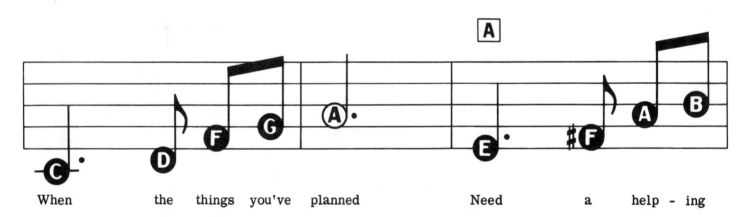

When the things you've planned Need a help - ing

hand, I will un - der - stand,

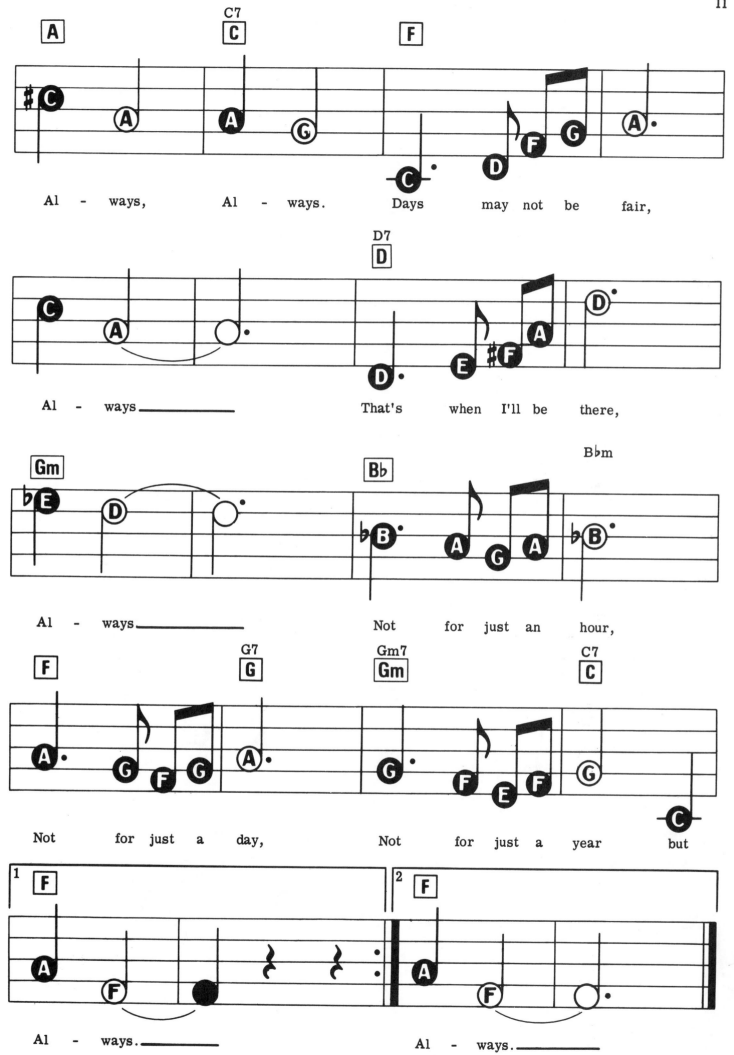

And I Love Her

Registration 8
Rhythm: 8 Beat or Rock

Words and Music by John Lennon
and Paul McCartney

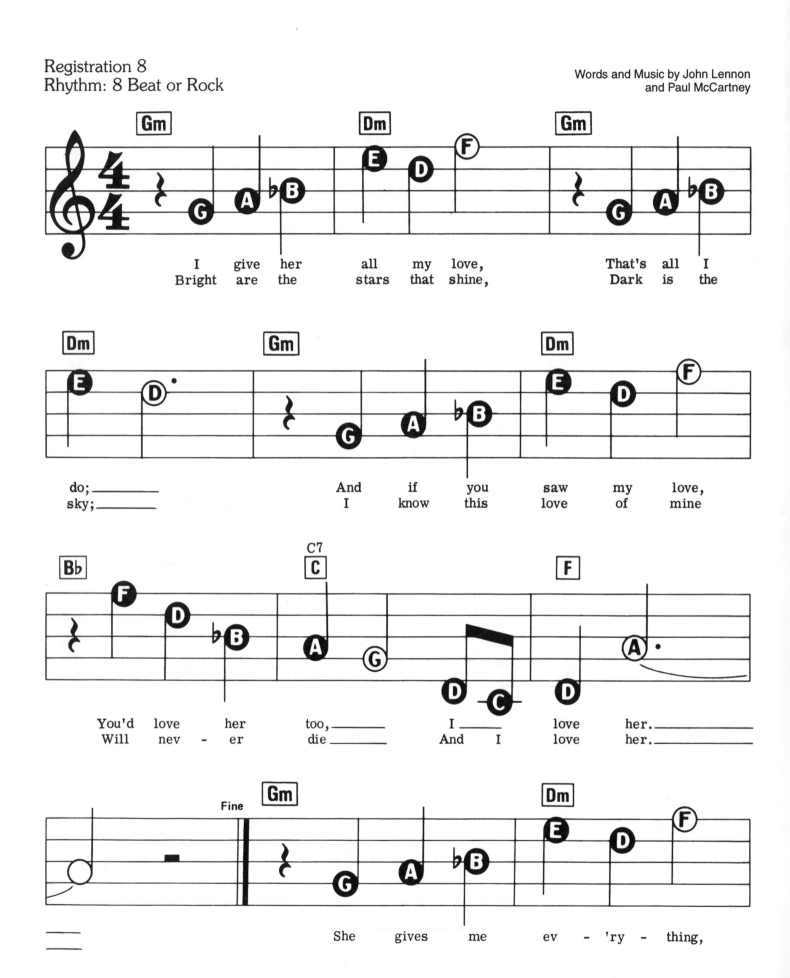

I give her all my love,
Bright are the stars that shine,

That's all I
Dark is the

do;
sky;

And if you saw my love,
I know this love of mine

You'd love her too,
Will nev - er die

I love her.
And I love her.

She gives me ev - 'ry - thing,

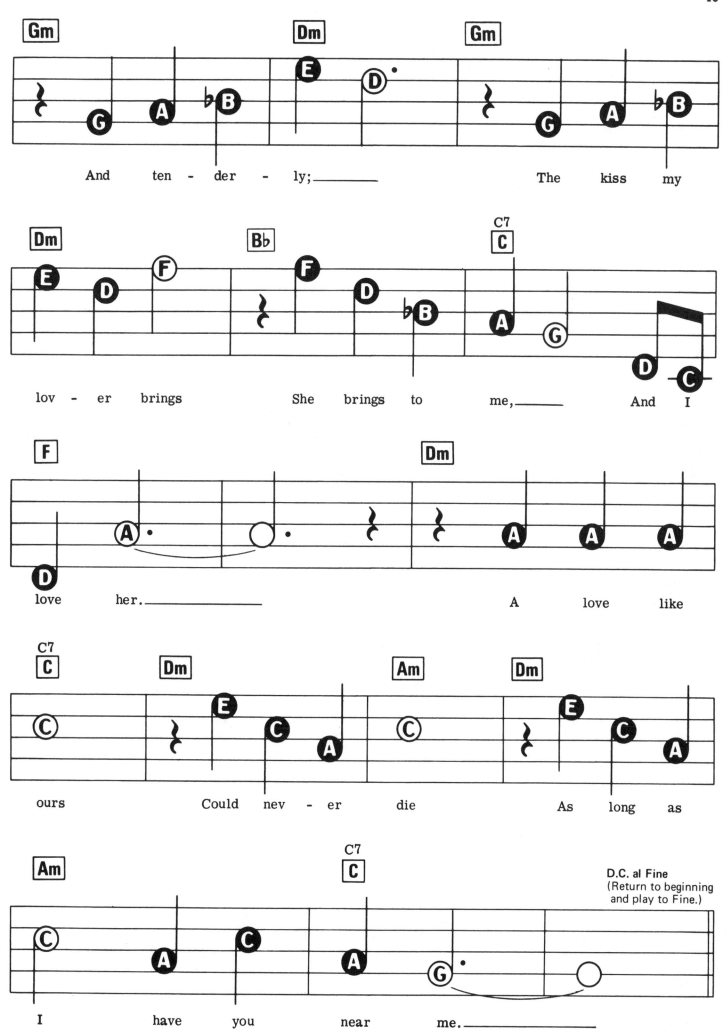

And So It Goes

Registration 10
Rhythm: Waltz

Words and Music by
Billy Joel

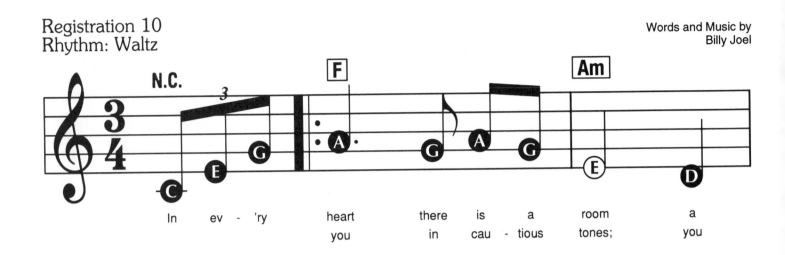

In ev - 'ry   heart   there   is   a   room   a
you   in   cau - tious   tones;   you

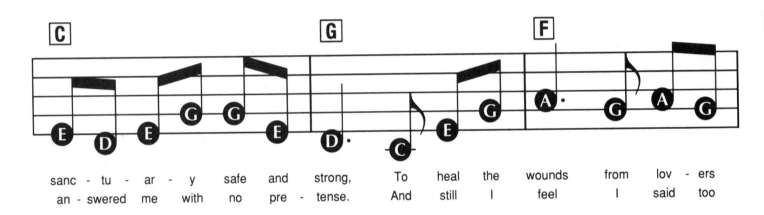

sanc - tu - ar - y   safe   and   strong,   To   heal   the   wounds   from   lov - ers
an - swered   me   with   no   pre - tense.   And   still   I   feel   I   said   too

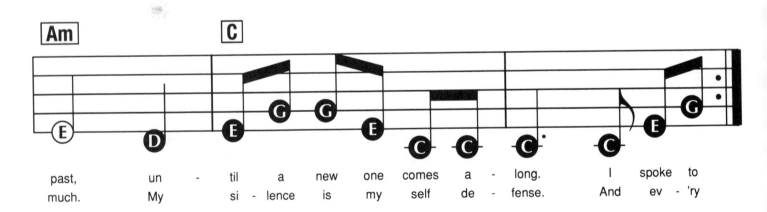

past,   un - til   a   new   one   comes   a - long.   I   spoke   to
much.   My   si - lence   is   my   self   de - fense.   And   ev - 'ry

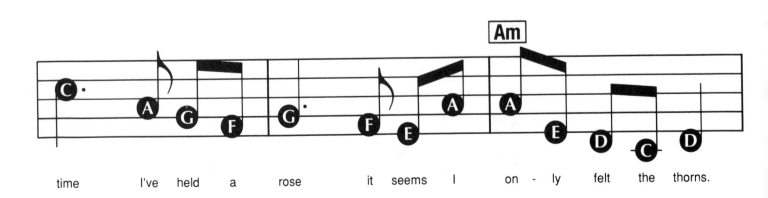

time   I've   held   a   rose   it   seems   I   on - ly   felt   the   thorns.

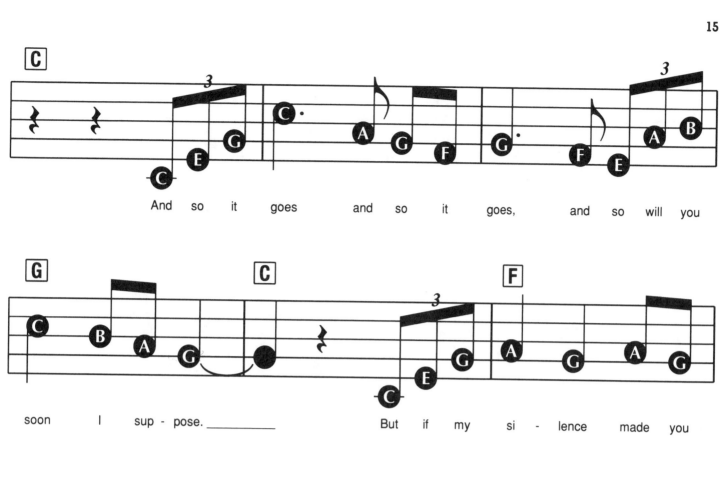

And so it goes and so it goes, and so will you

soon I sup - pose. _____ But if my si - lence made you

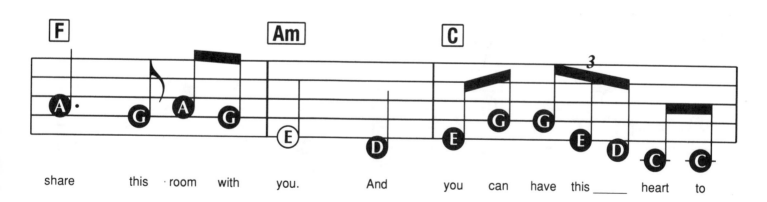

leave, then that would be my worst mis - take so I will

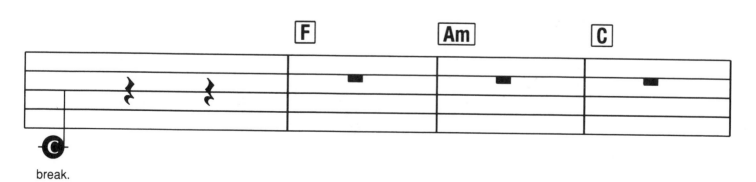

share this room with you. And you can have this _____ heart to

break.

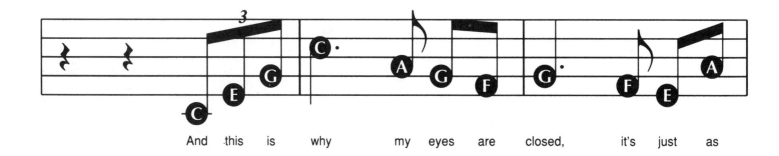

And this is why my eyes are closed, it's just as

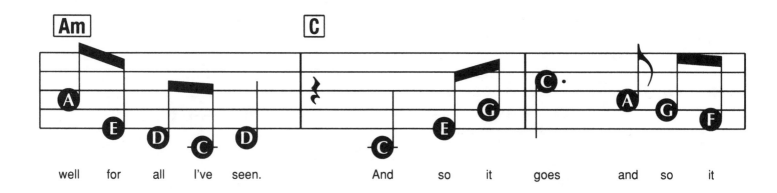

well for all I've seen. And so it goes and so it

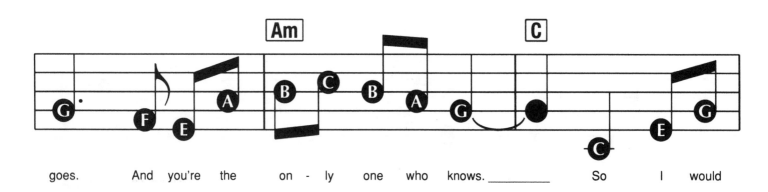

goes. And you're the on - ly one who knows. _____ So I would

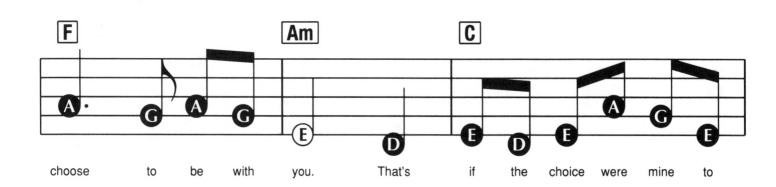

choose to be with you. That's if the choice were mine to

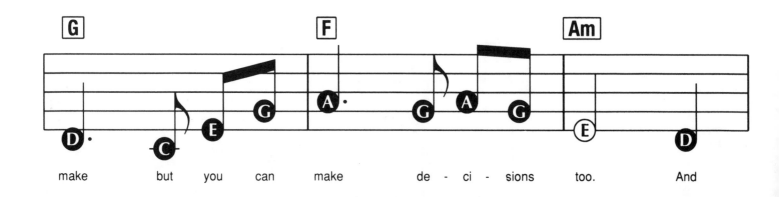

make but you can make de - ci - sions too. And

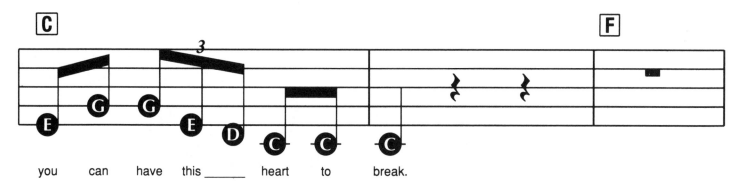

you can have this _____ heart to break.

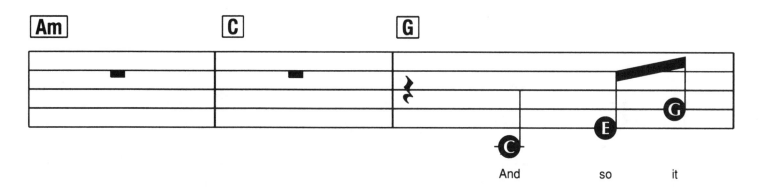

And so it

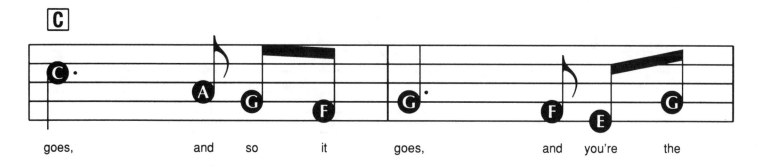

goes, and so it goes, and you're the

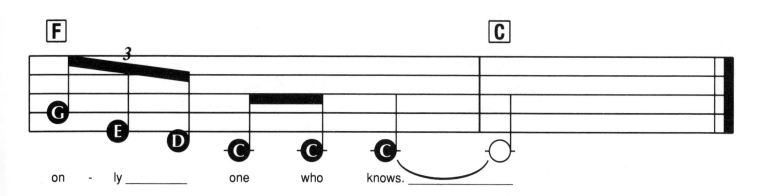

on - ly _____ one who knows. _____

Anytime You Need a Friend

Registration 4
Rhythm: 8-Beat or Rock

Words and Music by Mariah Carey
and Walter Afanasieff

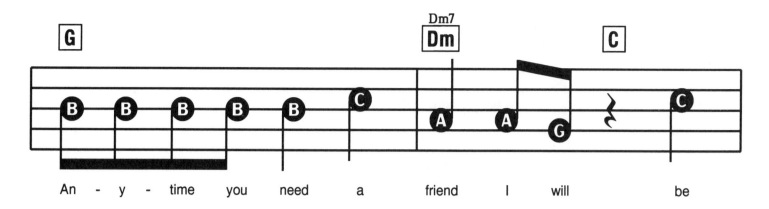

An - y - time you need a friend I will be

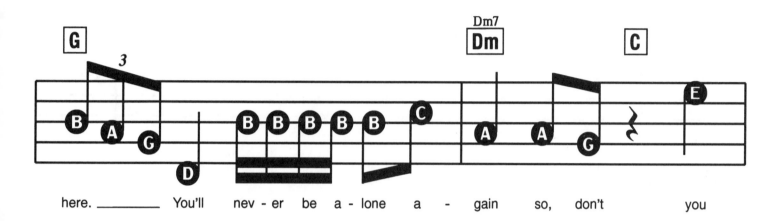

here. _____ You'll nev - er be a - lone a - gain so, don't you

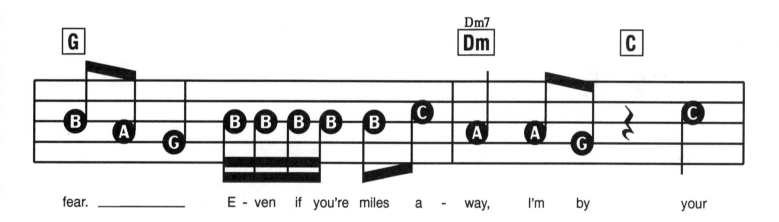

fear. _____ E - ven if you're miles a - way, I'm by your

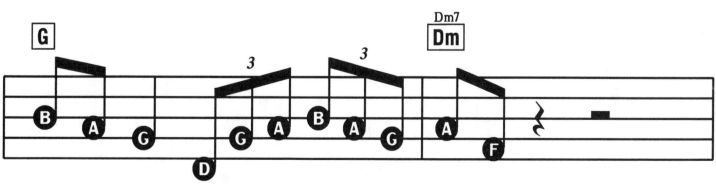

side. _____ So, don't you ev - er be lone - ly.

20

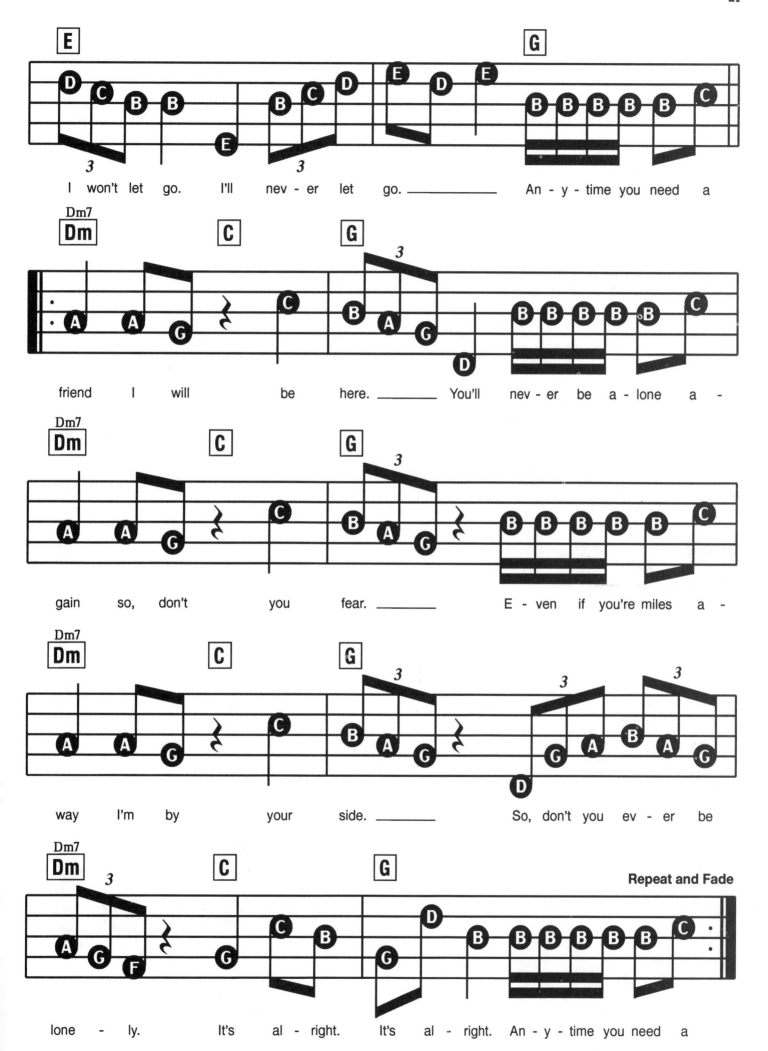

Bésame Mucho
(Kiss Me Much)

Music and Spanish Words by
Consuelo Velazquez
English Words by Sunny Skylar

Registration 1
Rhythm: Rhumba or Latin

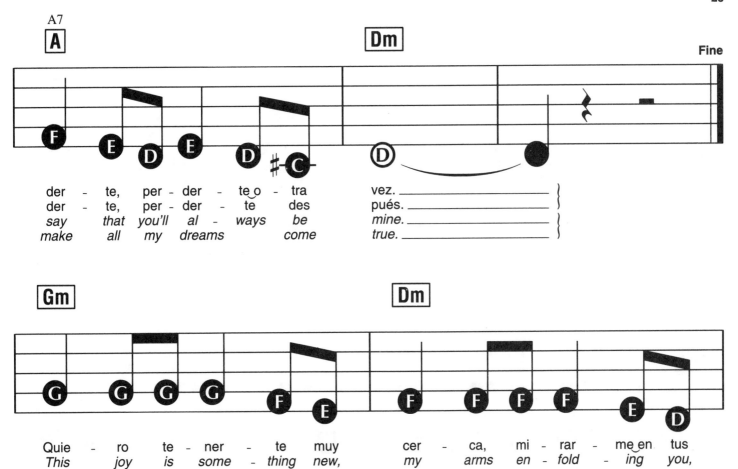

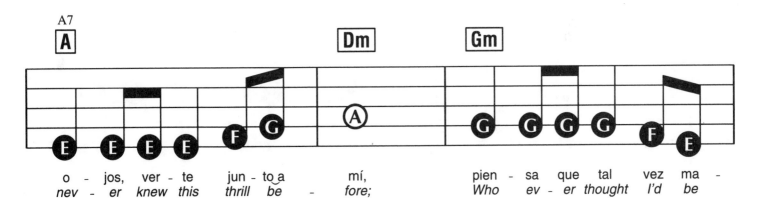

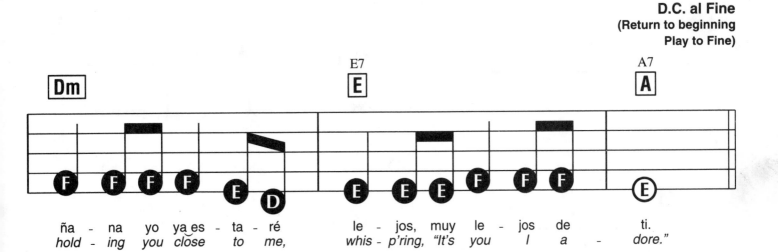

Cherish

Registration 3
Rhythm: Rock or Disco

Words and Music by
Terry Kirkman

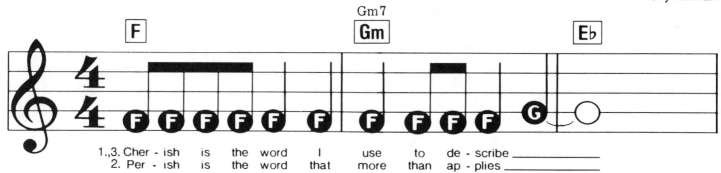

1.,3. Cher - ish is the word I use to de - scribe _____
2. Per - ish is the word that more than ap - plies _____

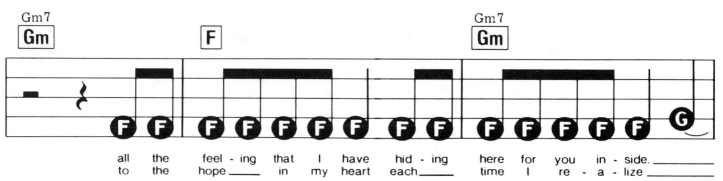

all the feel - ing that I have hid - ing here for you in - side. _____
to the hope _____ in my heart each _____ time I re - a - lize _____

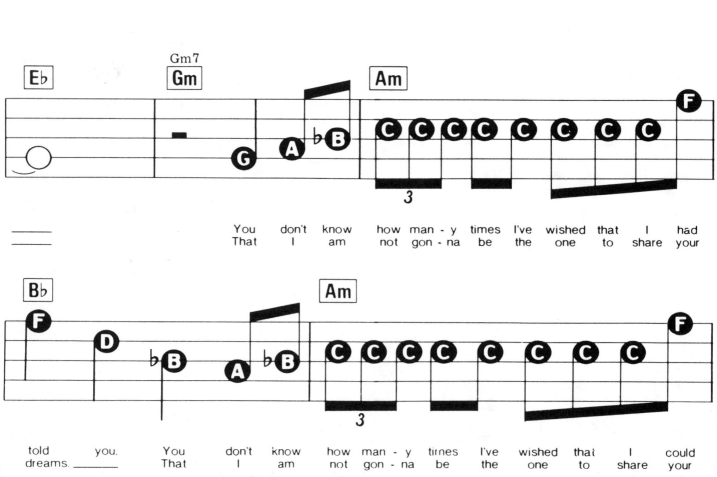

_____ You don't know how man - y times I've wished that I had
_____ That I am not gon - na be the one to share your

told you. You don't know how man - y times I've wished that I could
dreams. _____ That I am not gon - na be the one to share your

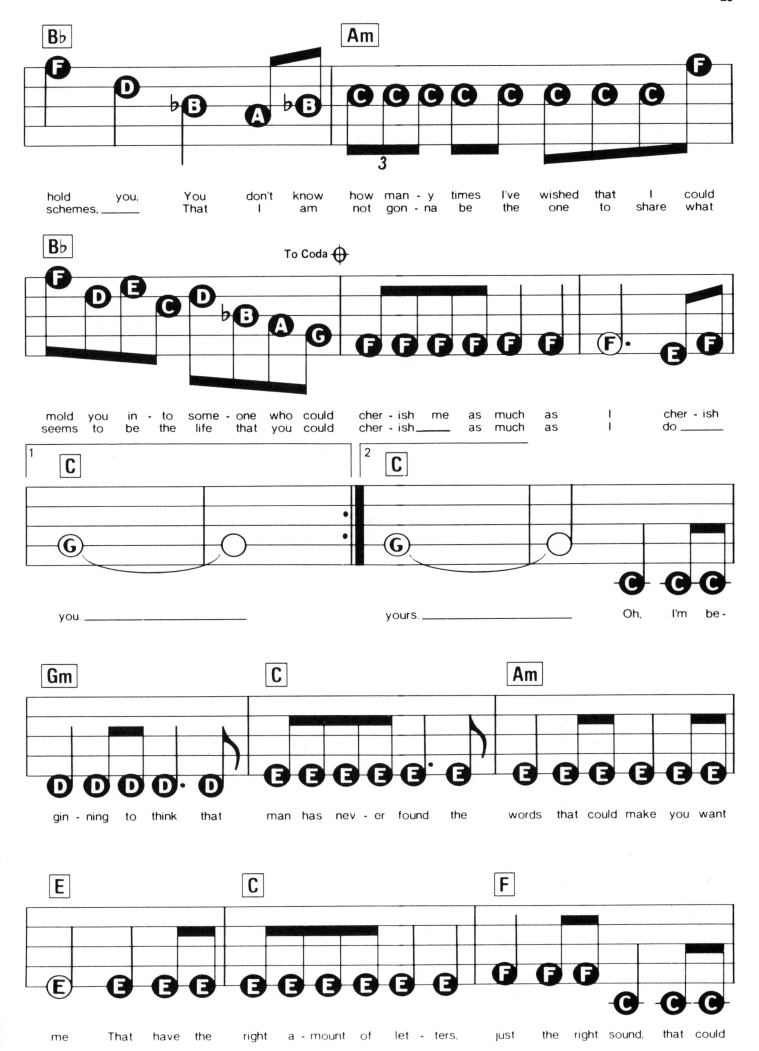

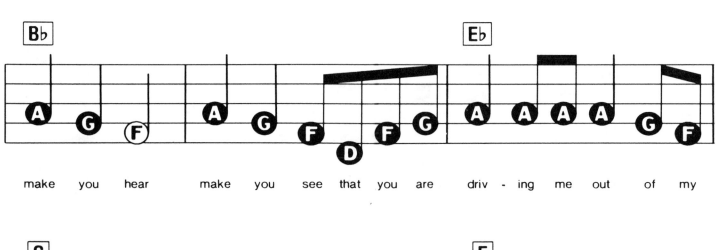

make you hear make you see that you are driv - ing me out of my

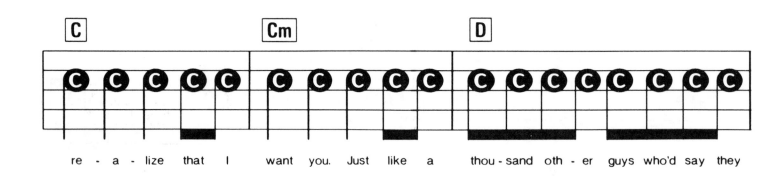

mind. _____ Oh, I could say I need you, but then you'd

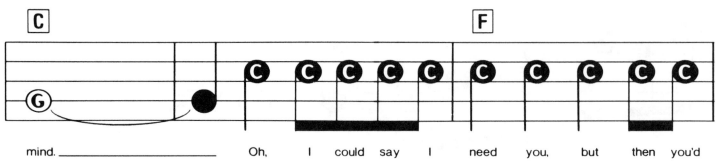

re - a - lize that I want you. Just like a thou - sand oth - er guys who'd say they

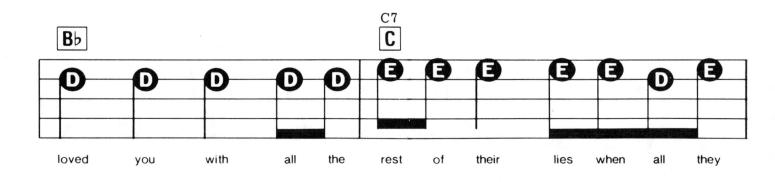

loved you with all the rest of their lies when all they

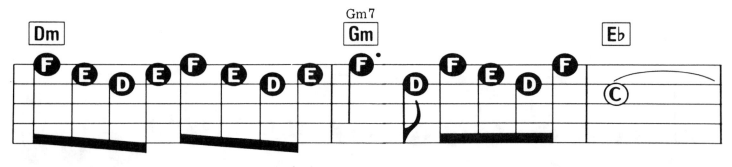

want - ed was to touch your face, your hands and gaze in - to your eyes. _____

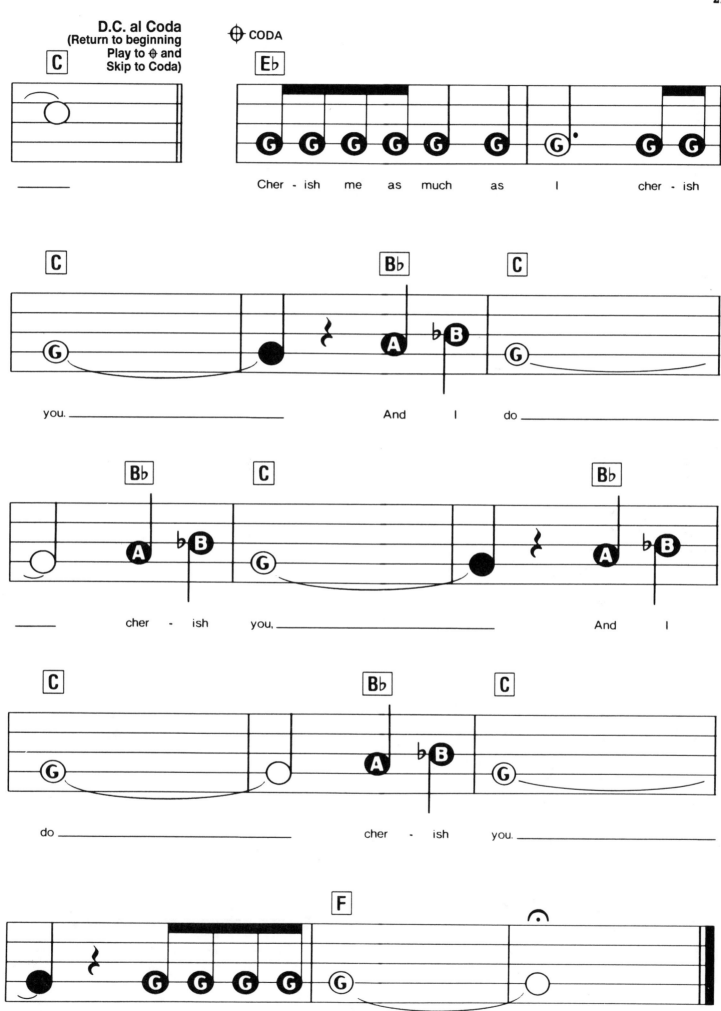

(They Long to Be)
Close to You

Registration 2
Rhythm: Slow Rock

Lyric by Hal David
Music by Burt Bacharach

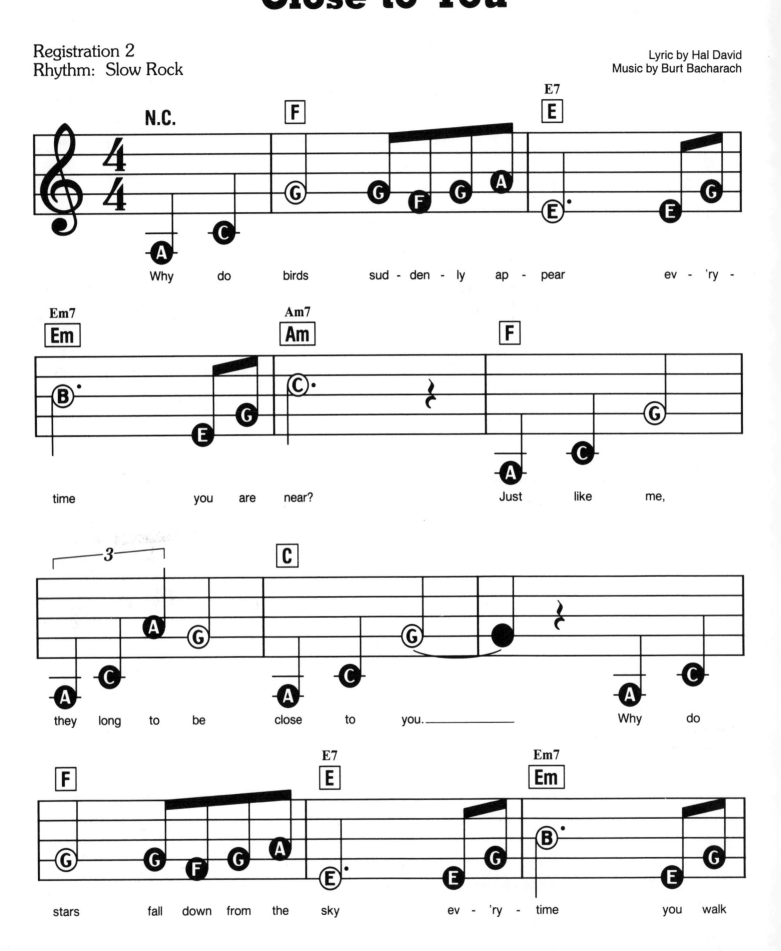

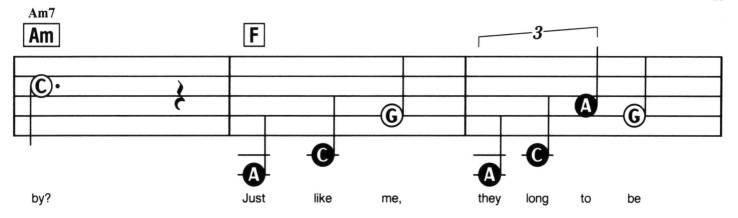

by?   Just   like   me,   they   long   to   be

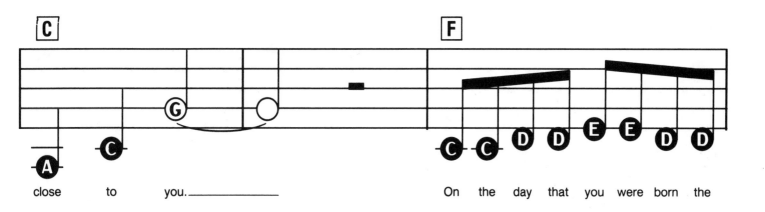

close   to   you._____   On   the   day   that   you   were   born   the

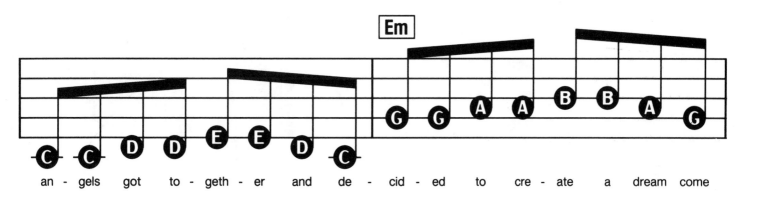

an - gels   got   to - geth - er   and   de - cid - ed   to   cre - ate   a   dream   come

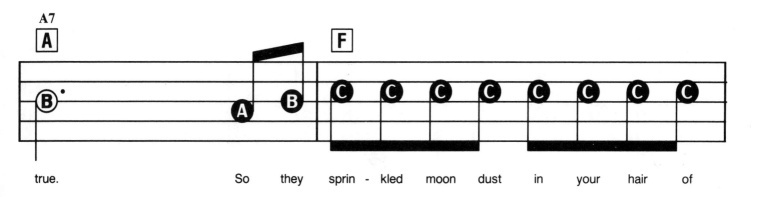

true.   So   they   sprin - kled   moon   dust   in   your   hair   of

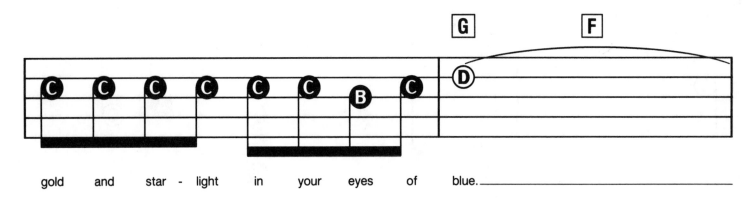

gold and star - light in your eyes of blue._____

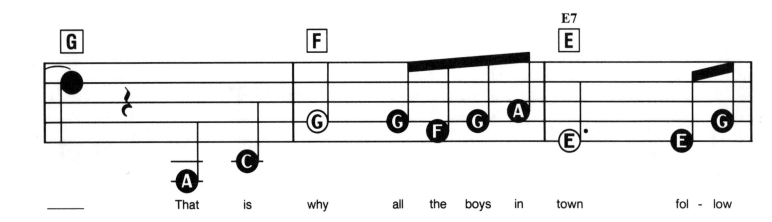

_____ That is why all the boys in town fol - low

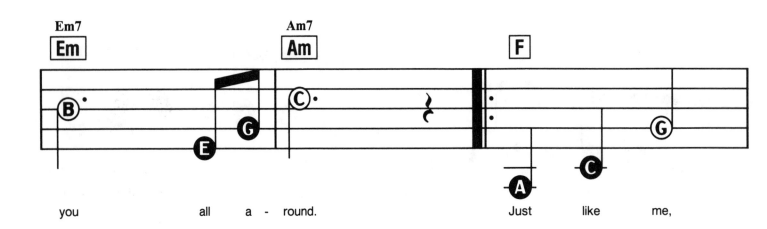

you all a - round. Just like me,

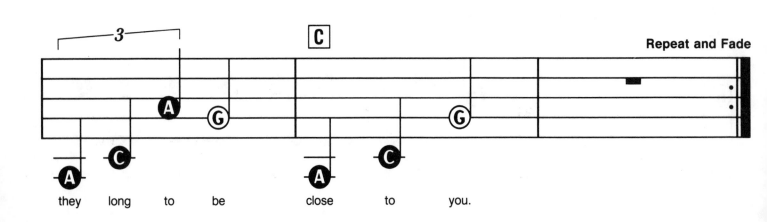

they long to be close to you.

Ev'ry Time We Say Goodbye
from SEVEN LIVELY ARTS

Registration 1
Rhythm: Latin or Bossa Nova

Words and Music by
Cole Porter

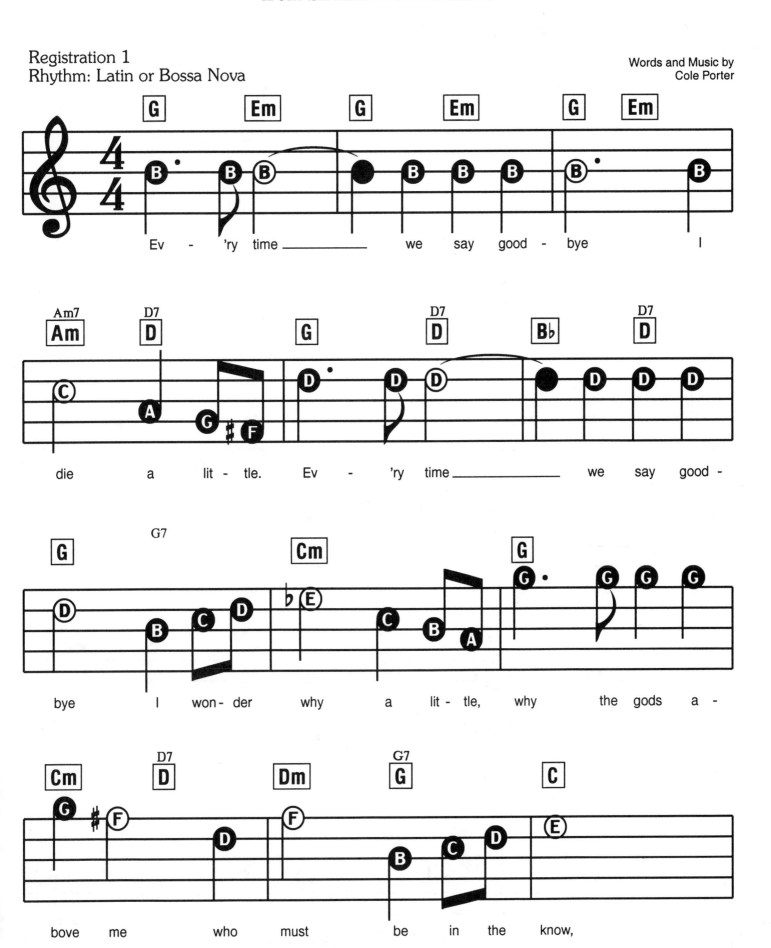

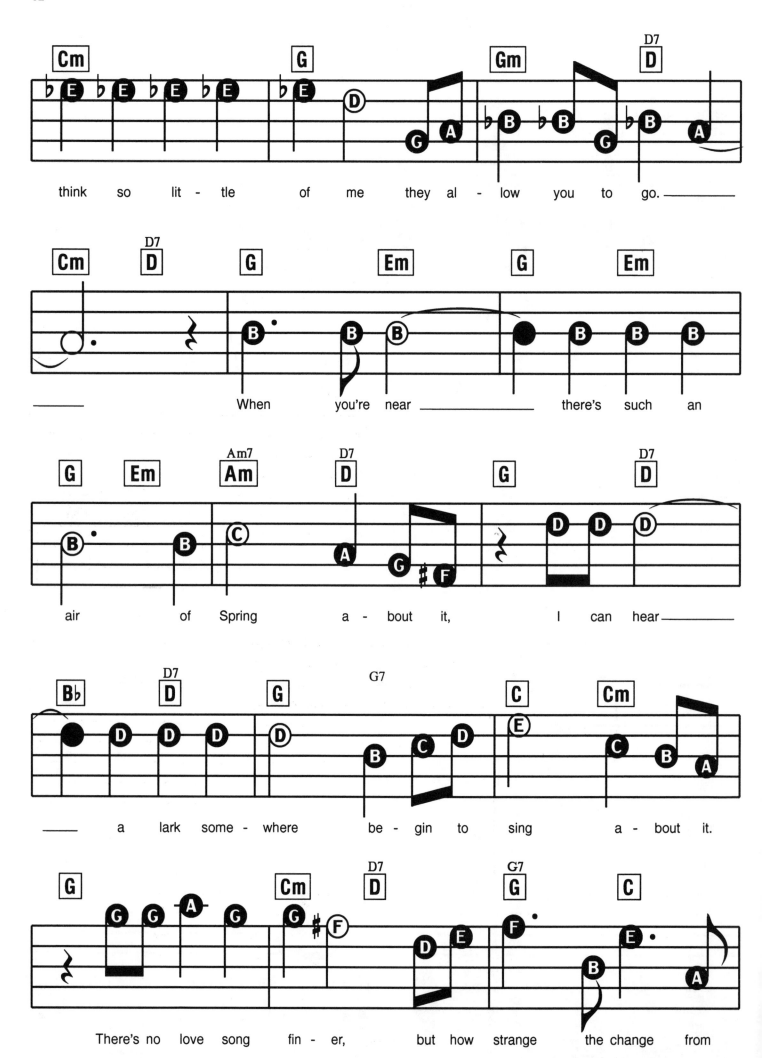

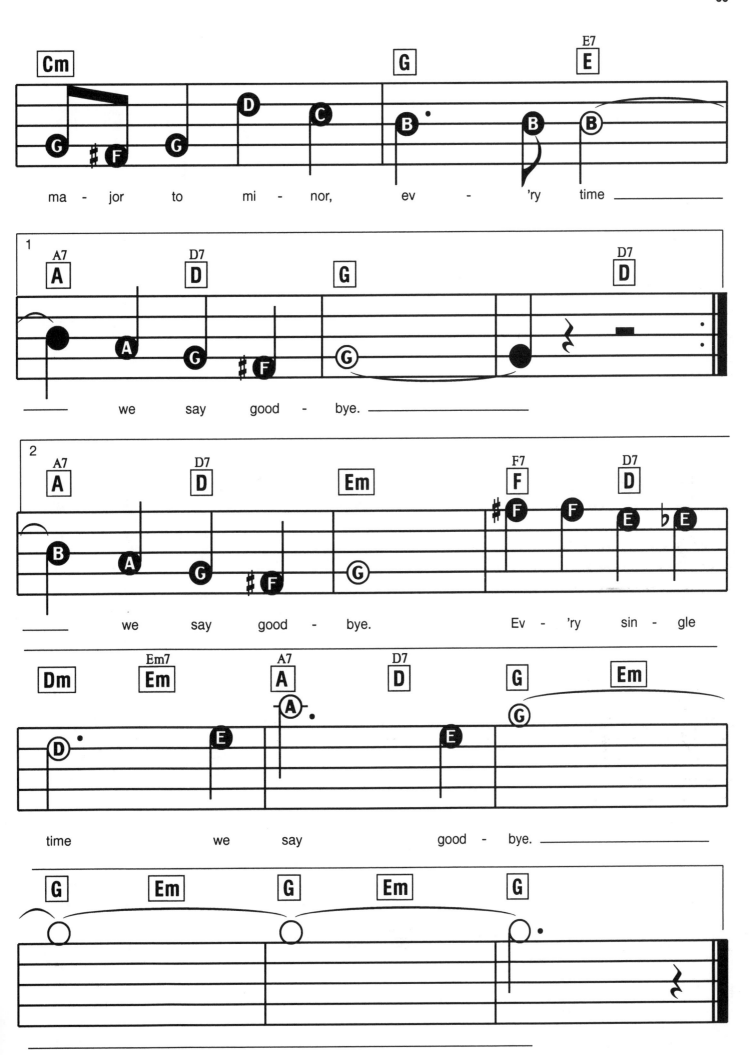

Do I Love You Because You're Beautiful?

from CINDERELLA

Registration 2
Rhythm: Ballad or Slow Rock

Lyrics by Oscar Hammerstein II
Music by Richard Rodgers

Do I love you be-cause you're beau-ti-ful? _____

_____ Or are you beau-ti-ful _____ be-cause I

love you? _____ Am I mak-ing be-lieve I

see in you _____ a girl too love-ly to _____

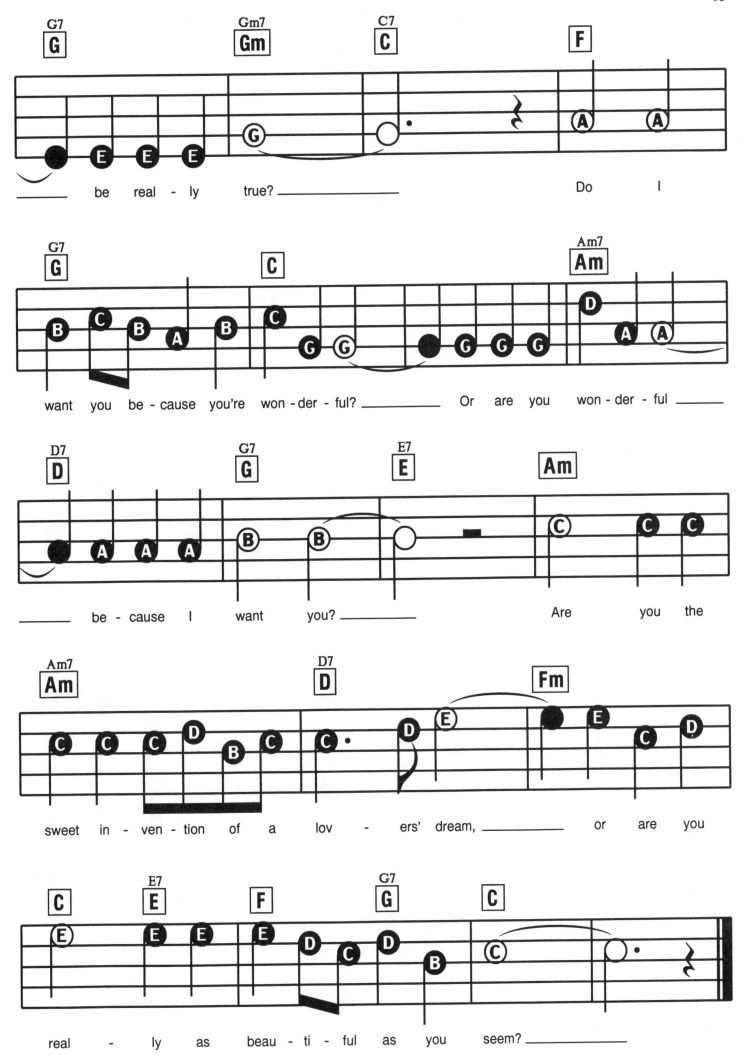

Everytime You Go Away

Registration 1
Rhythm: Rock or 8 Beat

Words and Music by
Daryl Hall

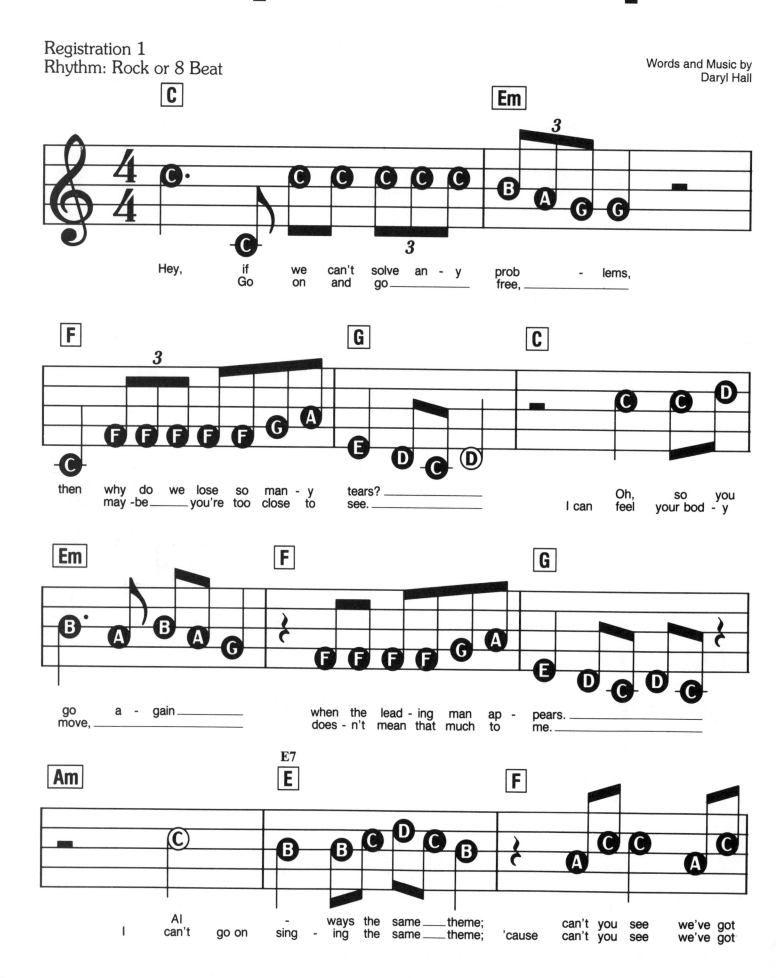

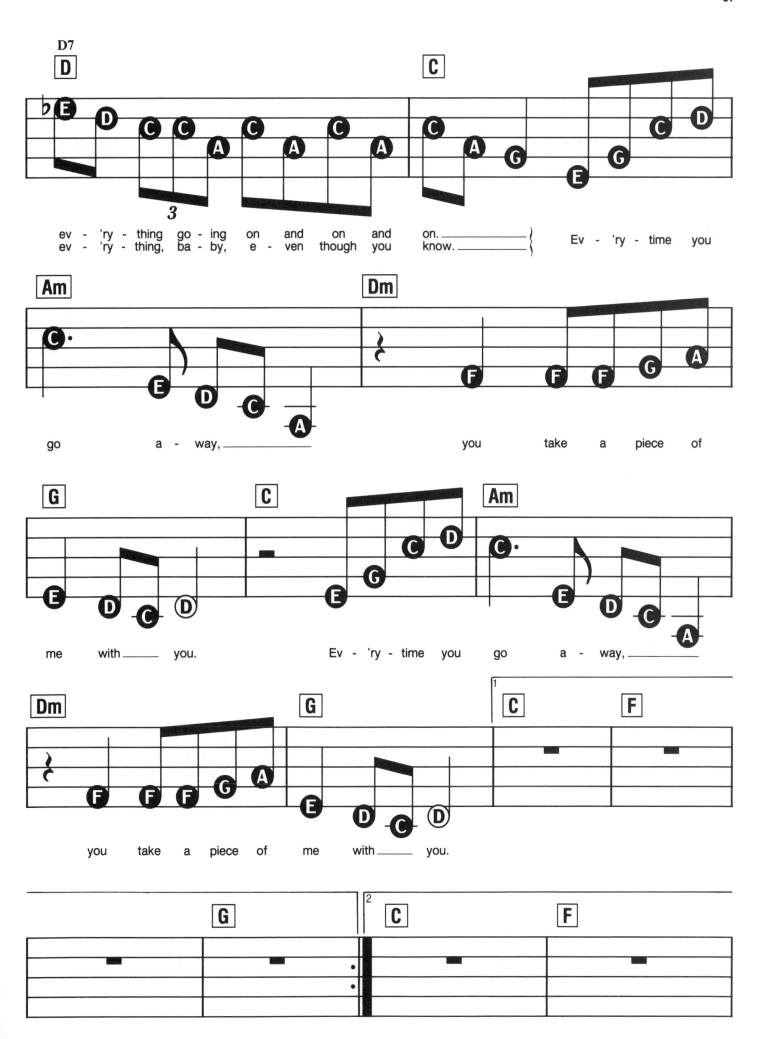

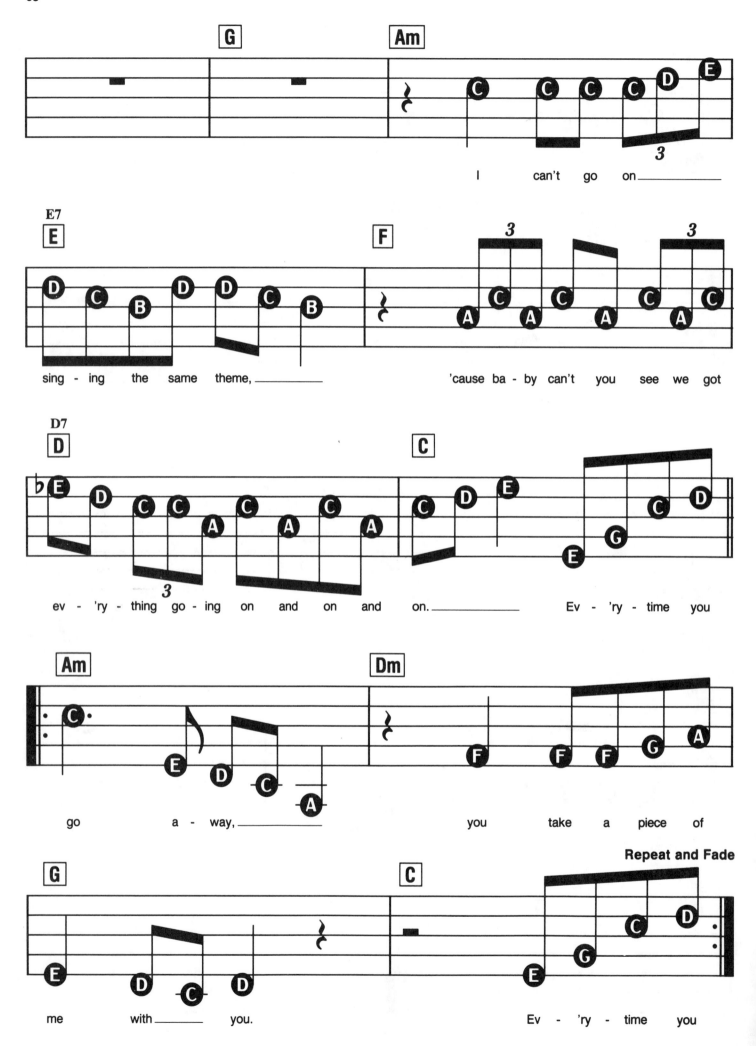

Feelings
(¿Dime?)

Registration 5
Rhythm: Slow Rock

English Words and Music by Morris Albert
and Louis Gaste
Spanish Words by Thomas Fundora

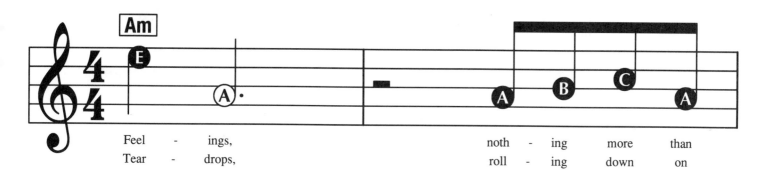

Feel - ings,   noth - ing   more   than
Tear - drops,   roll - ing   down   on

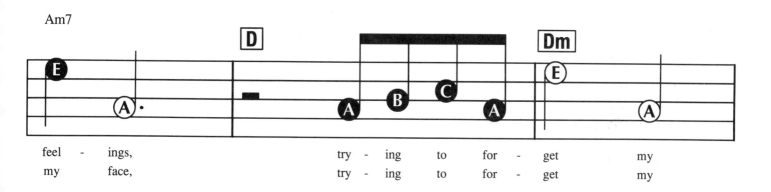

feel - ings,   try - ing   to   for - get   my
my   face,   try - ing   to   for - get   my

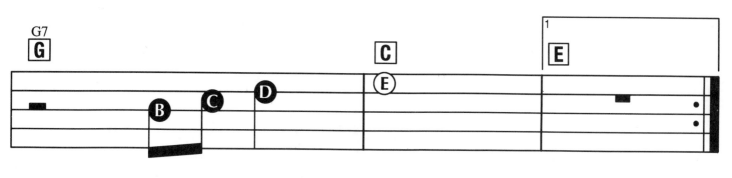

feel - ings   **of**   love.
feel - ings   **of**   love.

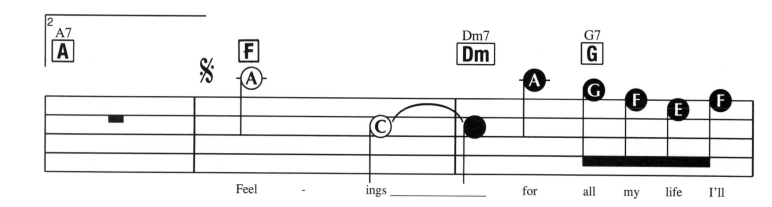

Feel - ings _____ for all my life I'll

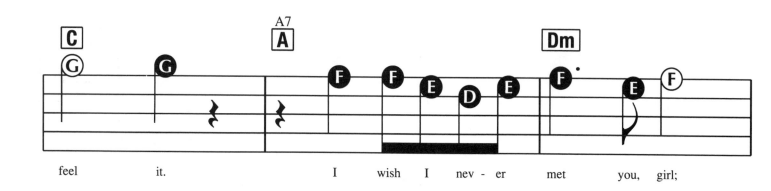

feel it. I wish I nev - er met you, girl;

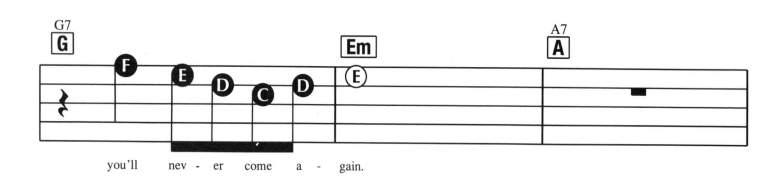

you'll nev - er come a - gain.

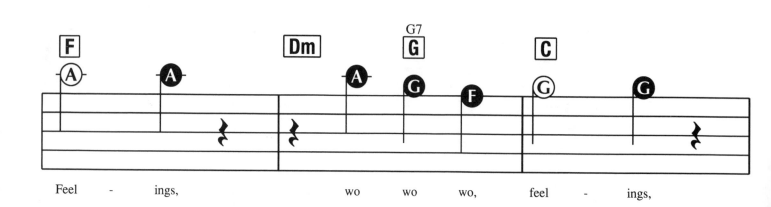

Feel - ings, wo wo wo, feel - ings,

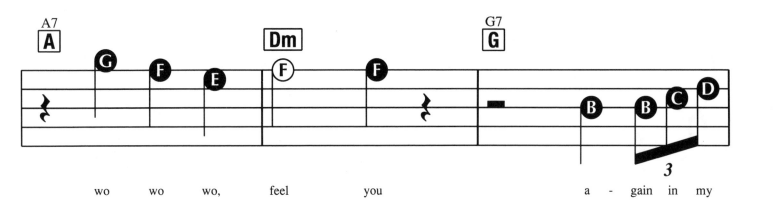

wo   wo   wo,   feel   you   a - gain in my

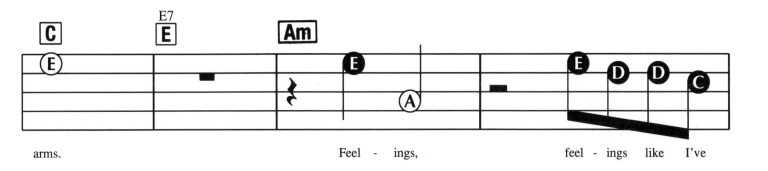

arms.   Feel - ings,   feel - ings like I've

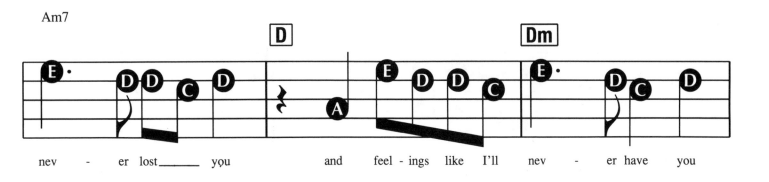

nev - er lost_____ you   and   feel - ings like I'll nev - er have you

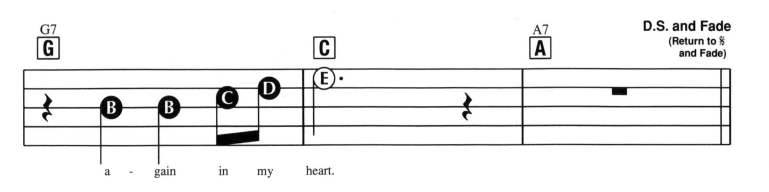

a - gain   in   my   heart.

D.S. and Fade
(Return to %
and Fade)

The First Time Ever I Saw Your Face

Registration 9
Rhythm: Ballad

Words and Music by
Ewan MacColl

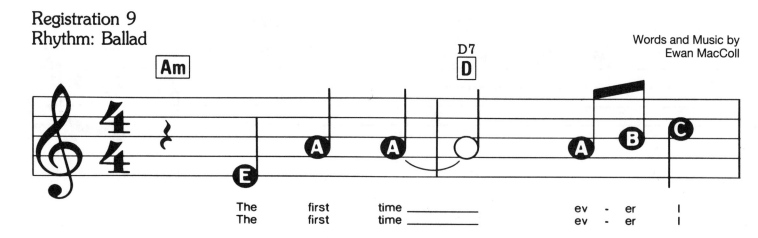

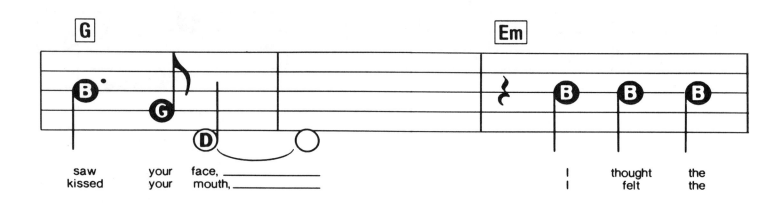

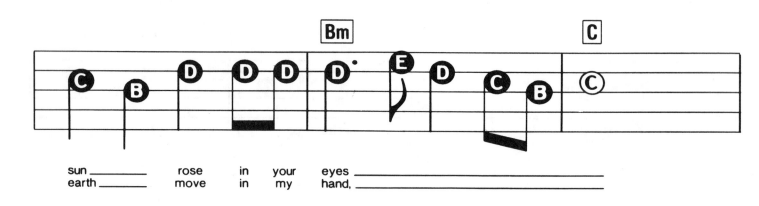

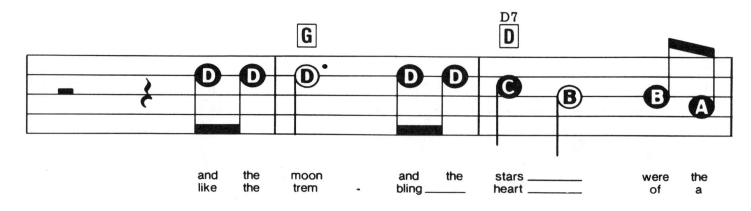

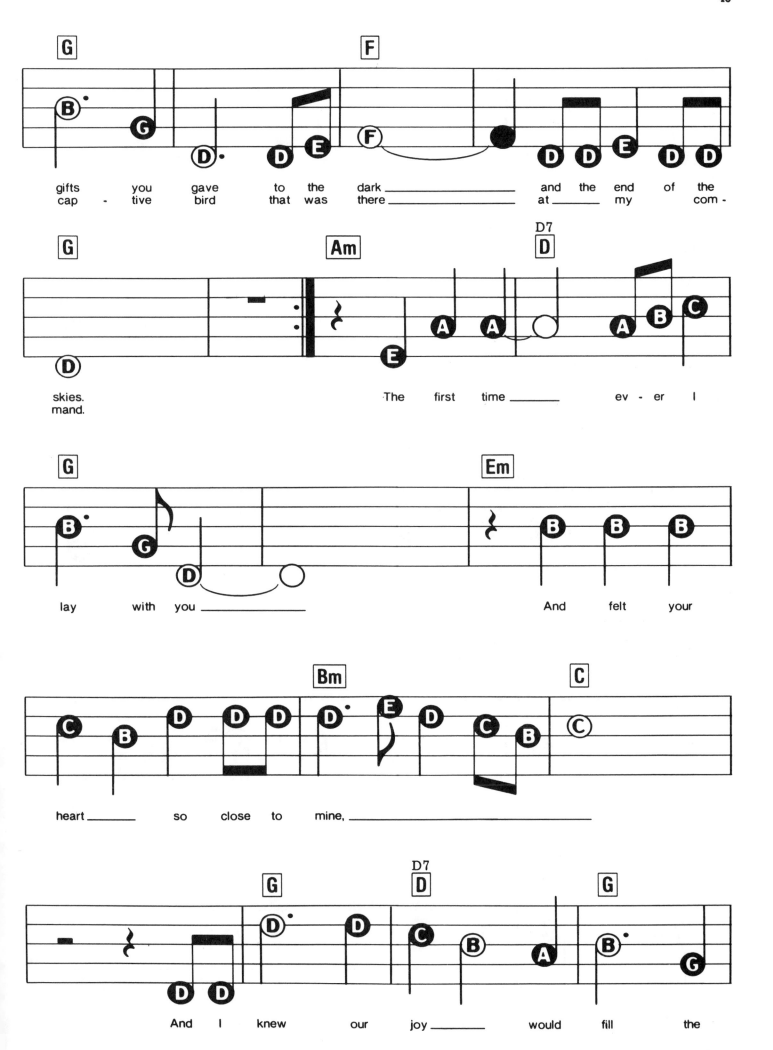

44

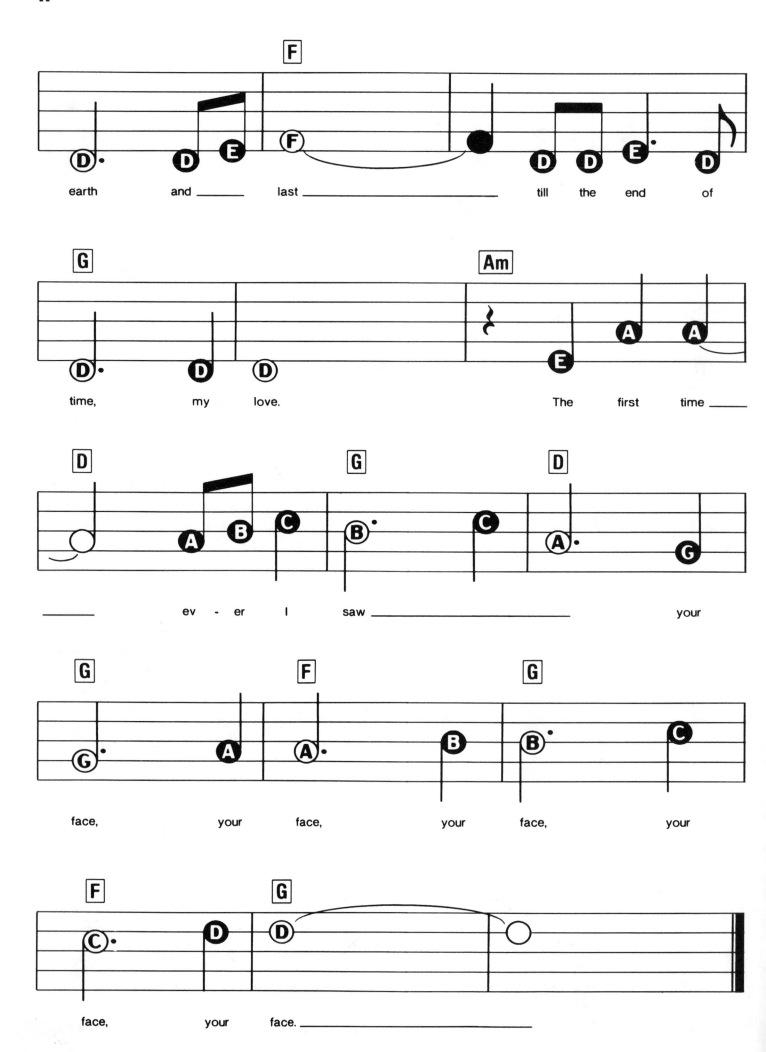

The Glory of Love
from GUESS WHO'S COMING TO DINNER

Registration 3
Rhythm: Swing or Big Band

Words and Music by
Billy Hill

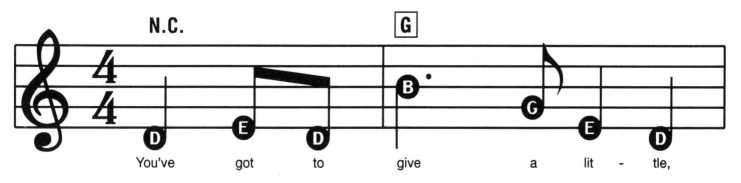

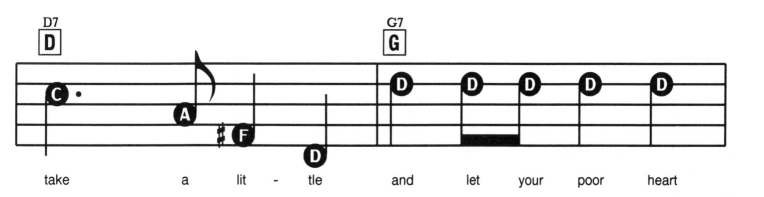

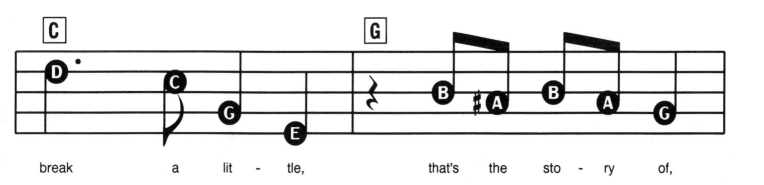

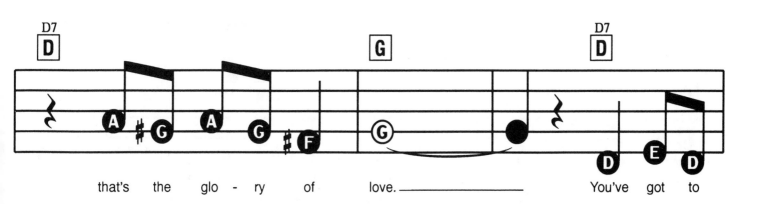

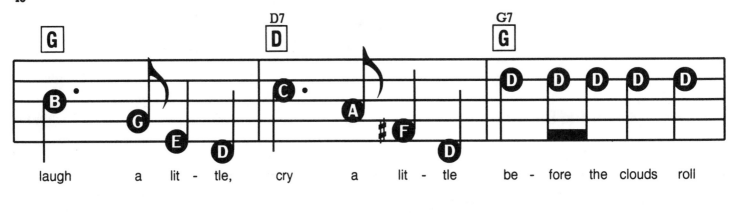

laugh a lit - tle, cry a lit - tle be - fore the clouds roll

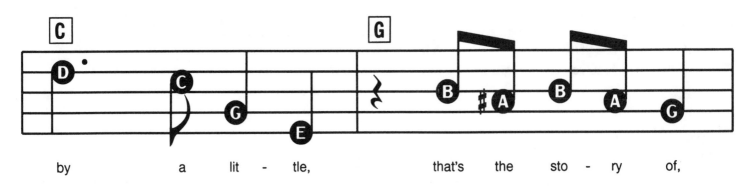

by a lit - tle, that's the sto - ry of,

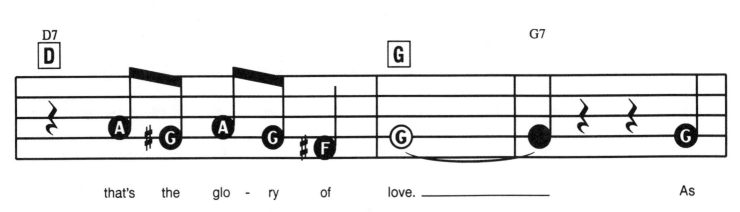

that's the glo - ry of love. _____ As

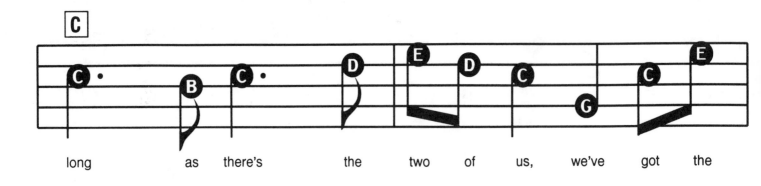

long as there's the two of us, we've got the

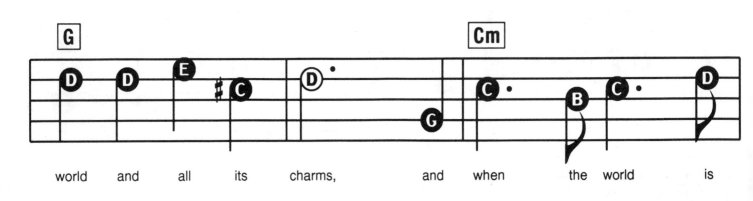

world and all its charms, and when the world is

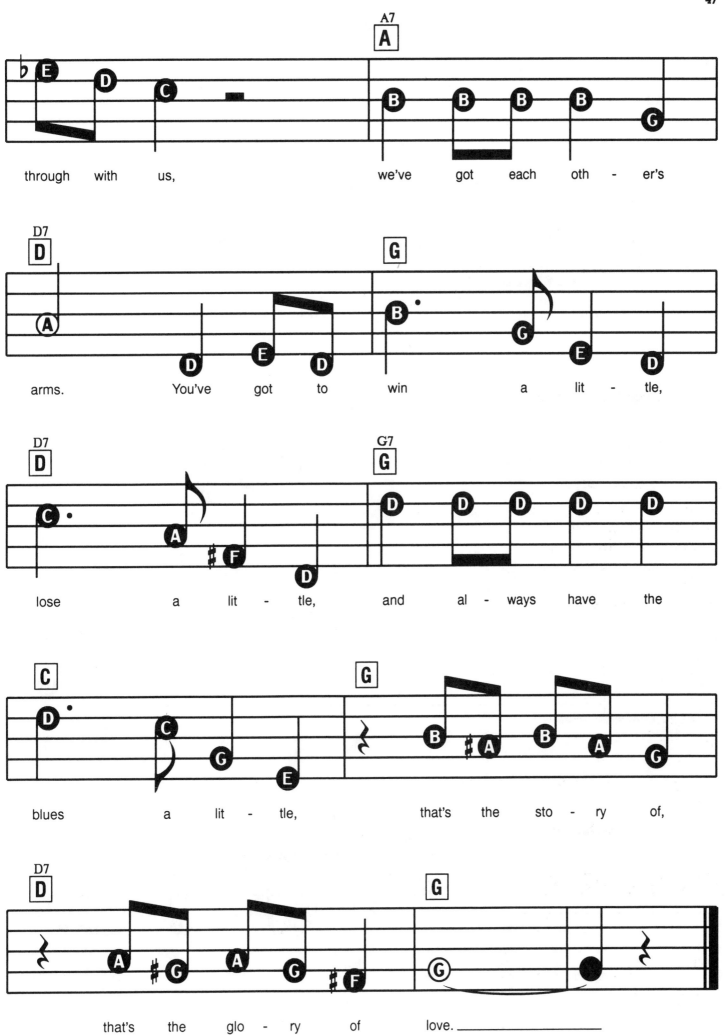

Friends

Registration 4
Rhythm: Rock

Words and Music by Michael W. Smith
and Deborah D. Smith

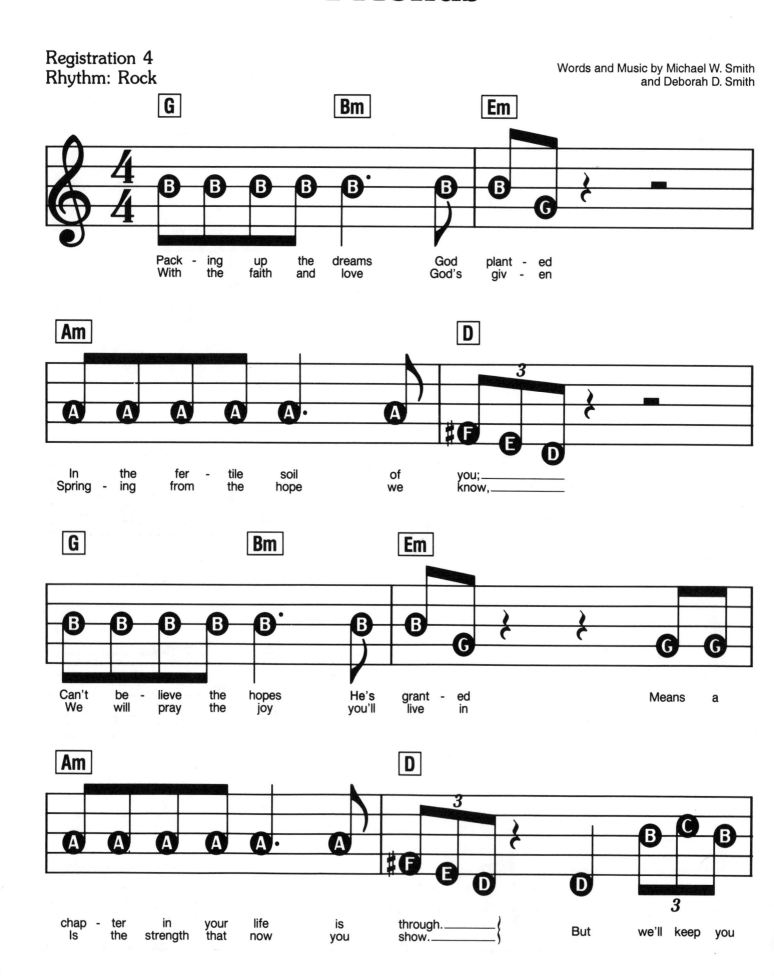

50

A Groovy Kind of Love

Registration 5
Rhythm: 8 Beat or Rock

Words and Music by Toni Wine
and Carole Bayer Sager

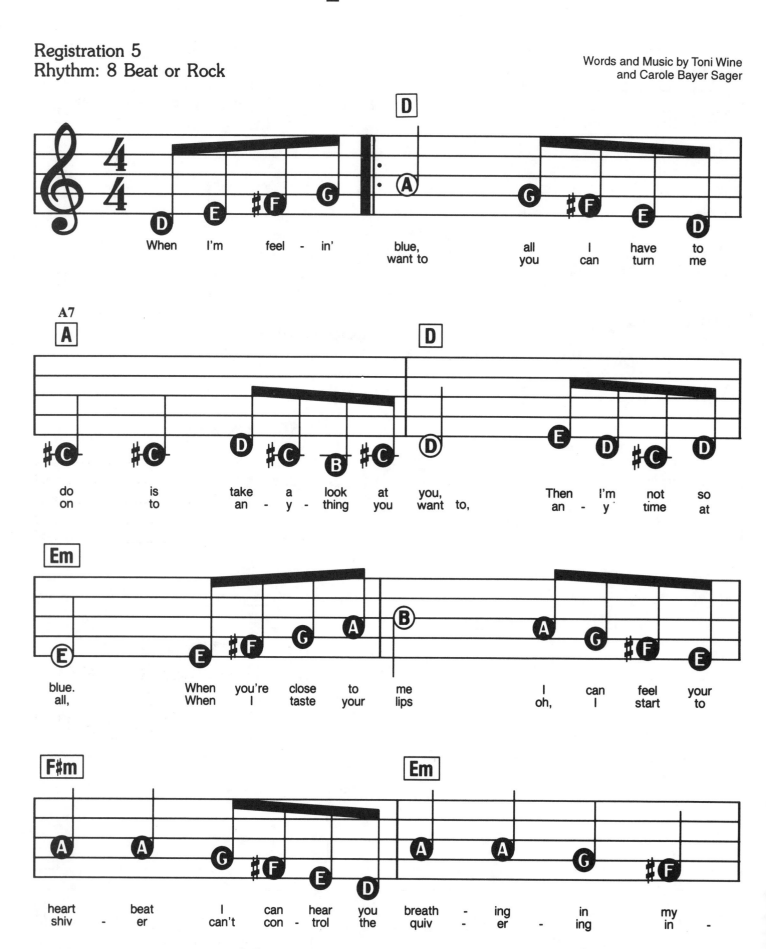

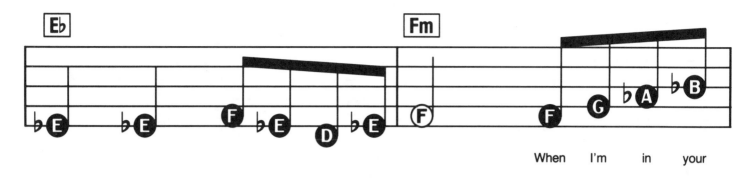

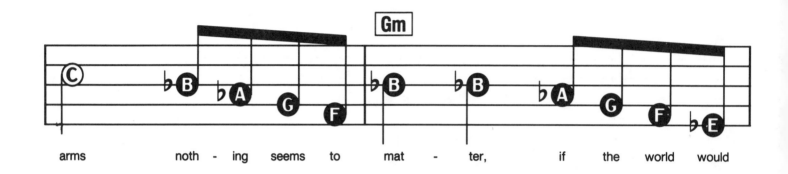

When I'm in your

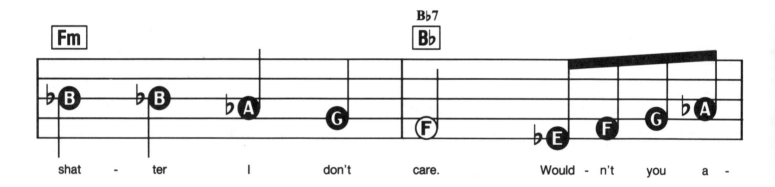

arms   noth - ing seems to   mat - ter,   if   the   world   would

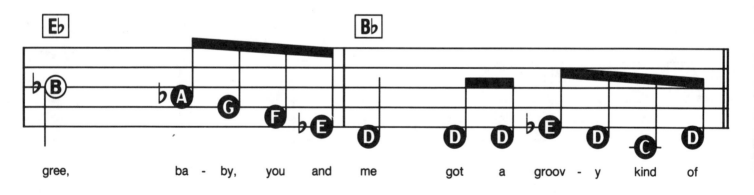

shat - ter   I   don't   care.   Would - n't   you   a -

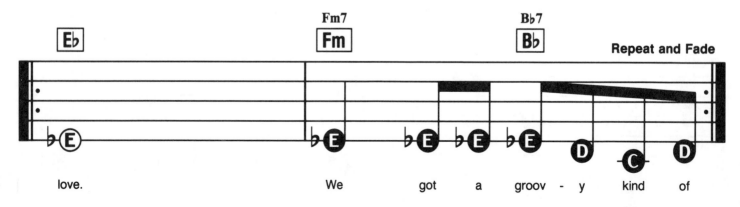

gree,   ba - by,   you   and   me   got   a   groov - y   kind   of

love.   We   got   a   groov - y   kind   of

I Will Be Here

Registration 8
Rhythm: Ballad

Words and Music by
Steven Curtis Chapman

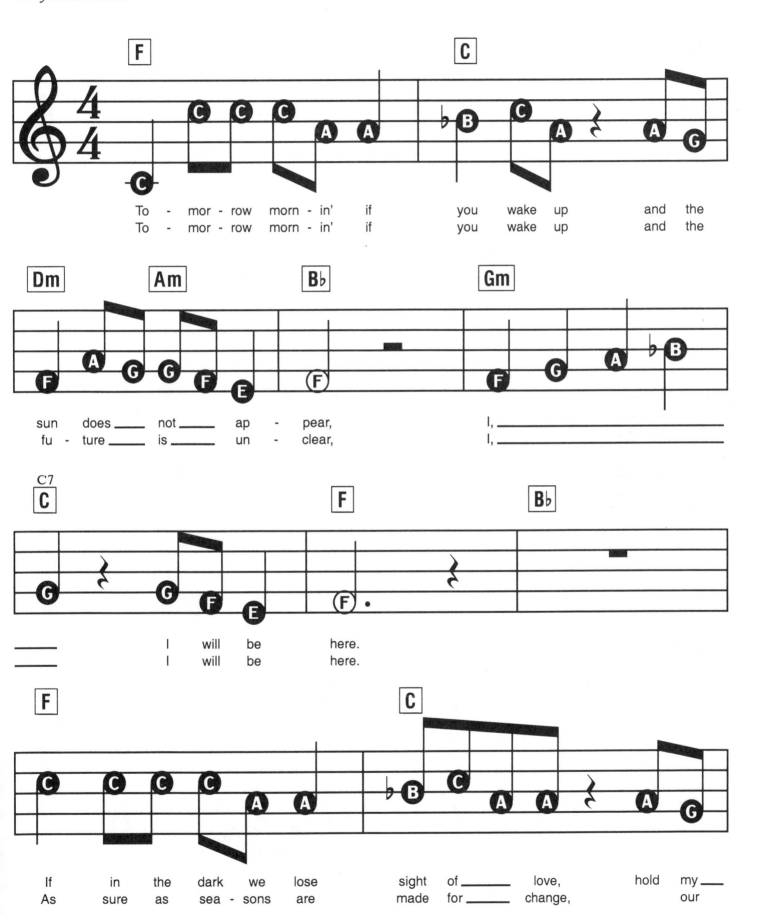

here.
here

When the laugh - ter turns _____ to
to watch you grow _____ in

cry - in' through the win - nin', los - in' and try - in', we'll be to -
beau - ty and tell you all the things you are to me. I will be

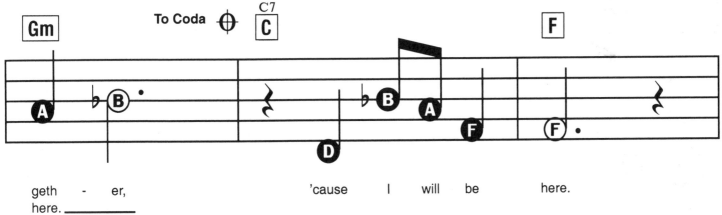

geth - er,
here. _____

'cause I will be here.

D.C. al Coda
(Return to beginning
Play to ⊕ and
Skip to Coda)

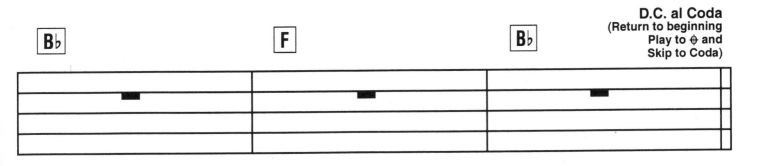

58

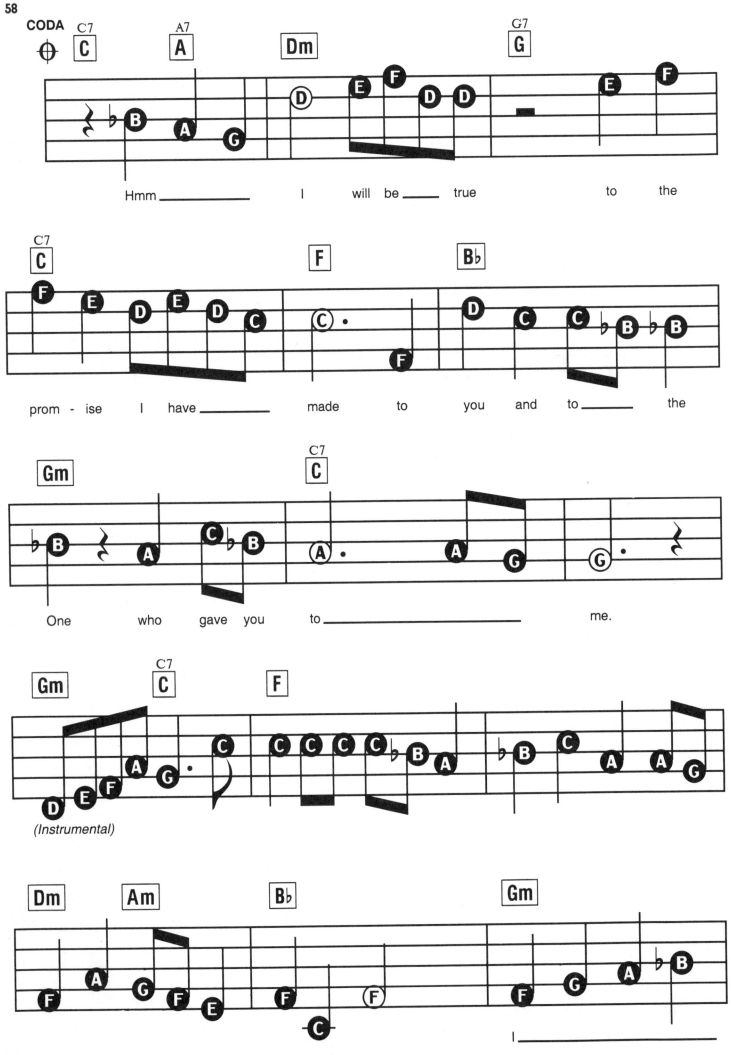

CODA

Hmm _____ I will be _____ true to the

prom - ise I have _____ made to you and to _____ the

One who gave you to _____ me.

(Instrumental)

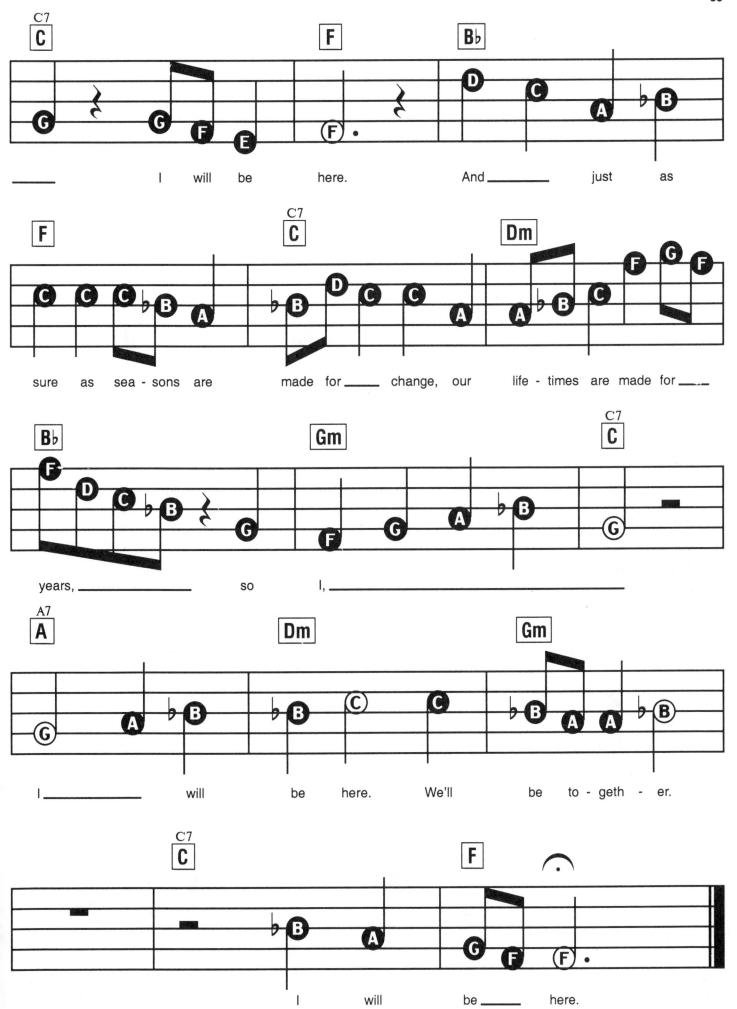

Grow Old with Me

Registration 7
Rhythm: Country Ballad

Words and Music by
John Lennon

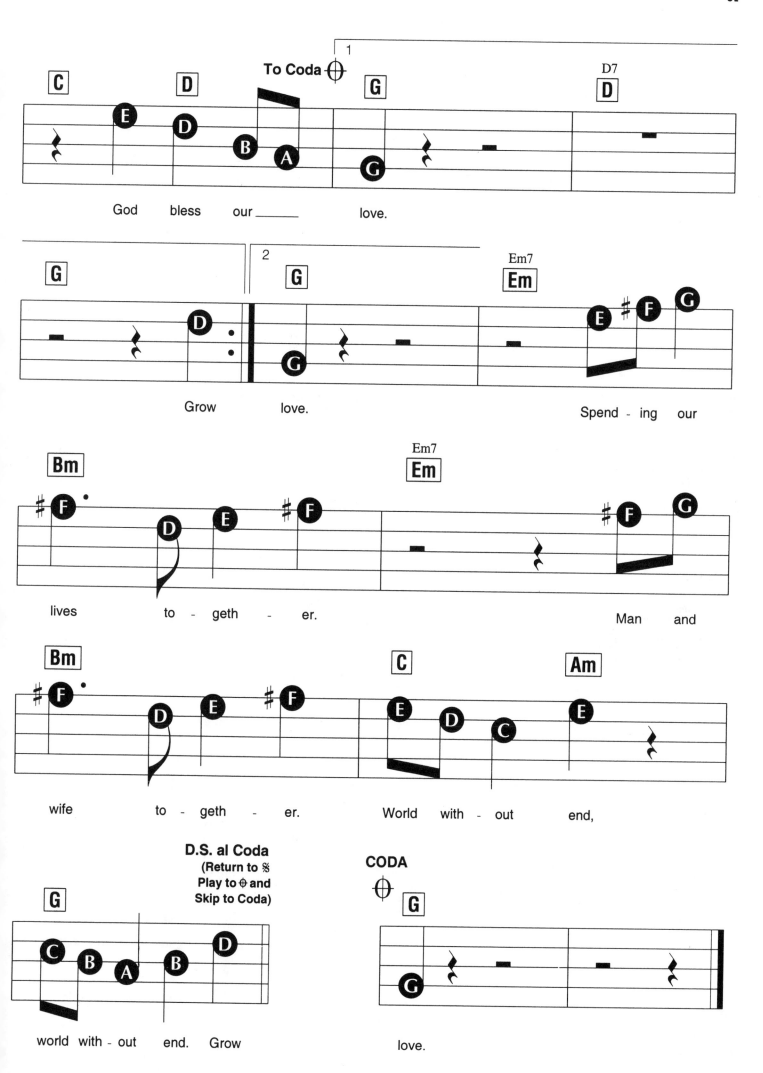

Here, There and Everywhere

Registration 2
Rhythm: 8 Beat or Rock

Words and Music by John Lennon
and Paul McCartney

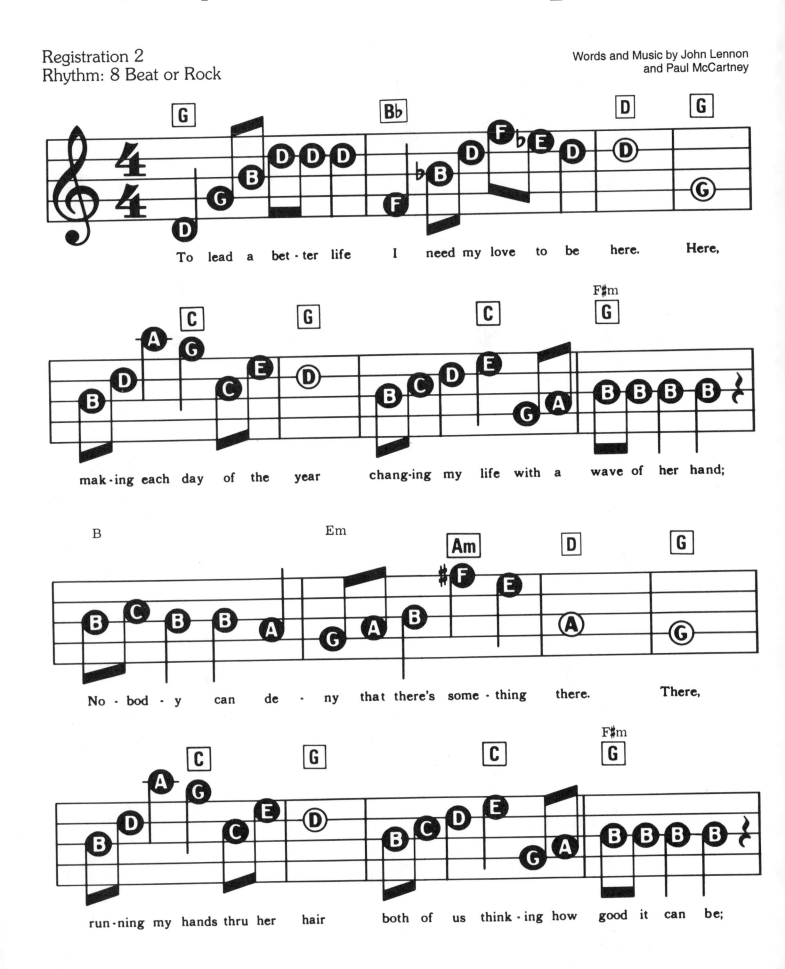

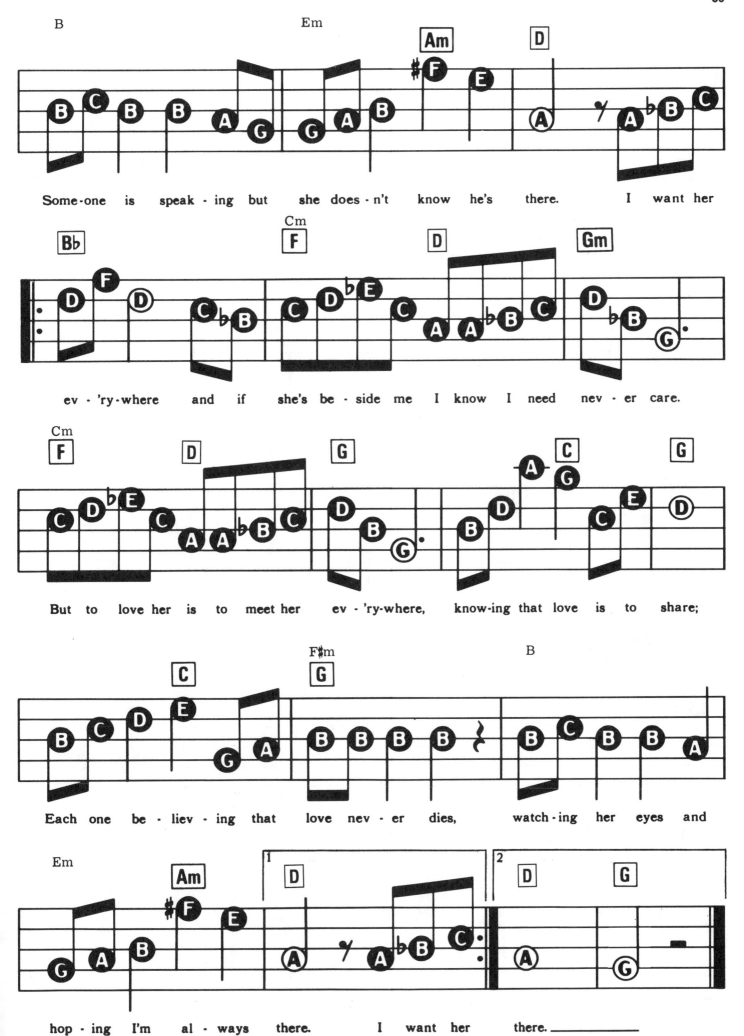

I Could Write a Book
from PAL JOEY

Registration 7
Rhythm: Fox Trot or Swing

Words by Lorenz Hart
Music by Richard Rodgers

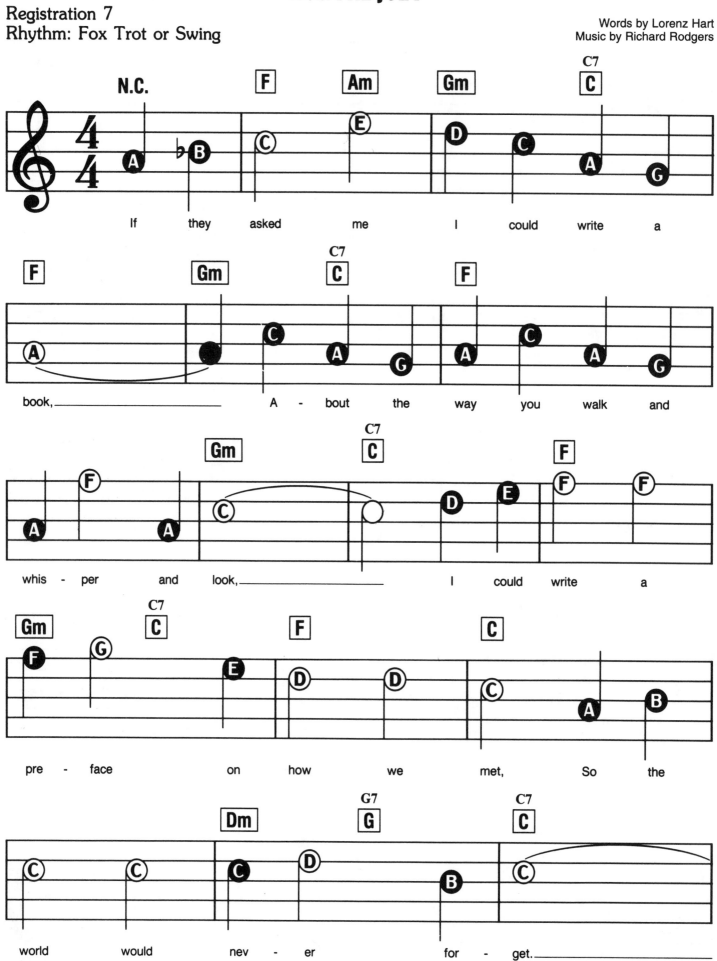

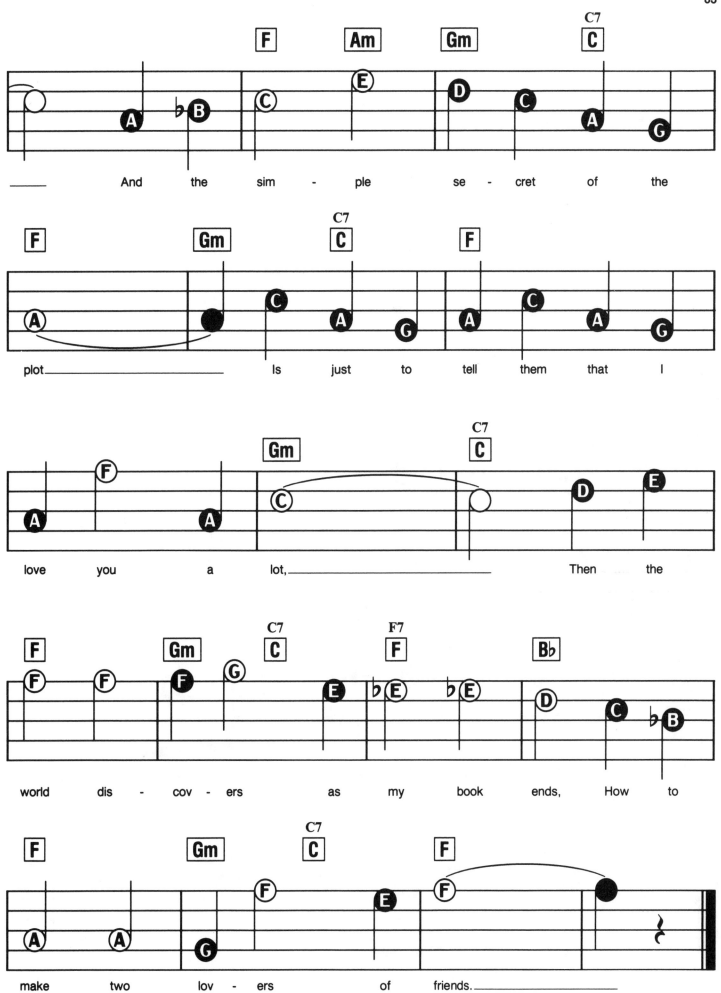

I Left My Heart in San Francisco

Registration 9
Rhythm: Fox Trot

Words by Douglas Cross
Music by George Cory

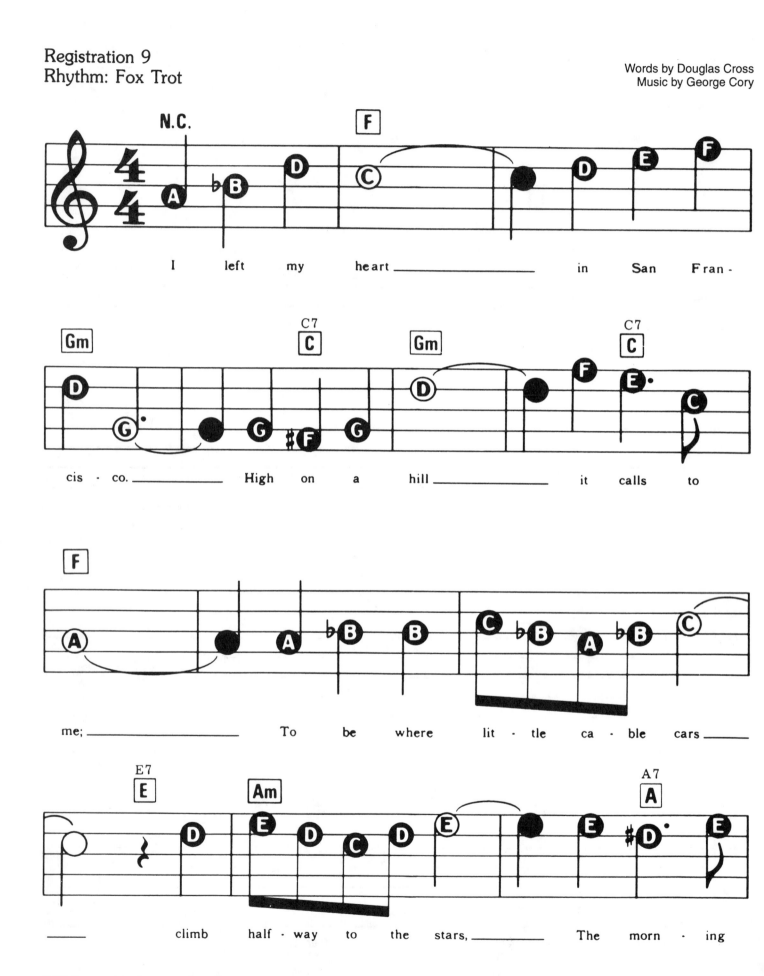

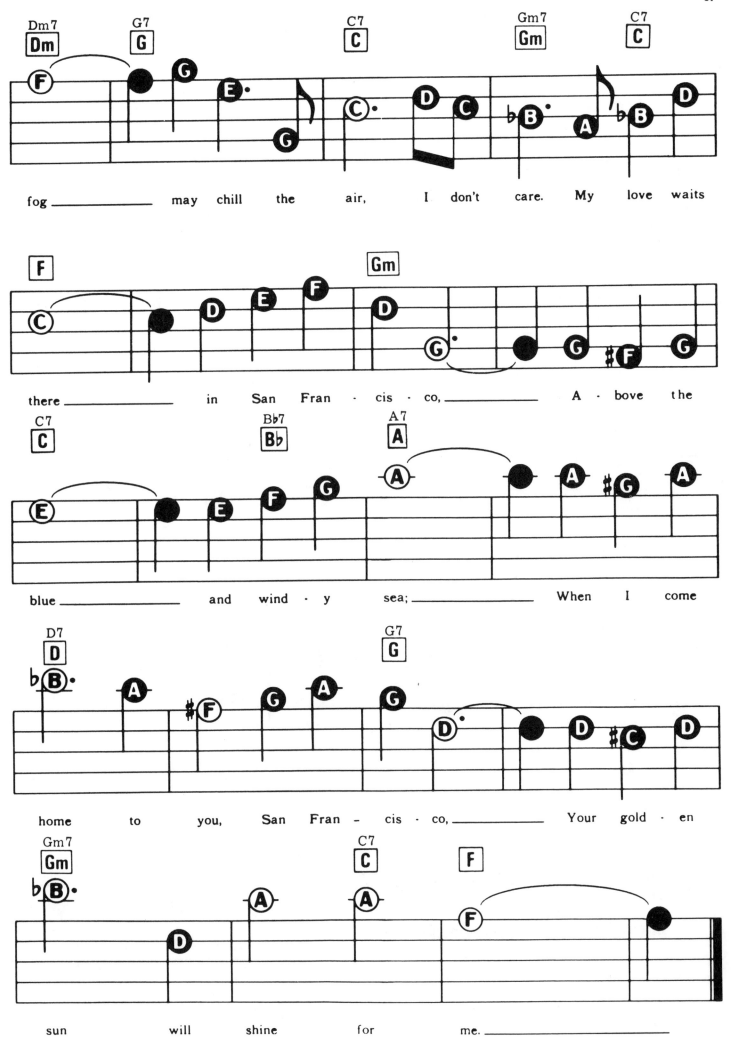

I'll Be There

Registration 9
Rhythm: Rock or 8 Beat

Words and Music by Berry Gordy, Hal Davis,
Willie Hutch and Bob West

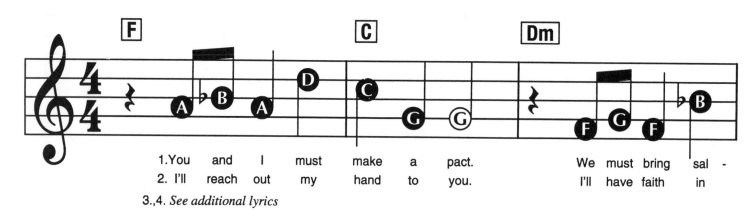

1. You and I must make a pact.
2. I'll reach out my hand to you.

We must bring sal i-

I'll have faith in

3.,4. *See additional lyrics*

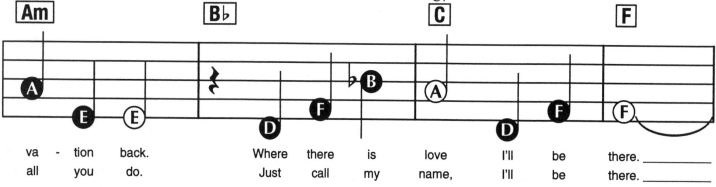

va - tion back.

all you do.

Where there is love,

Just call my name,

I'll be there. _____

I'll be there. _____

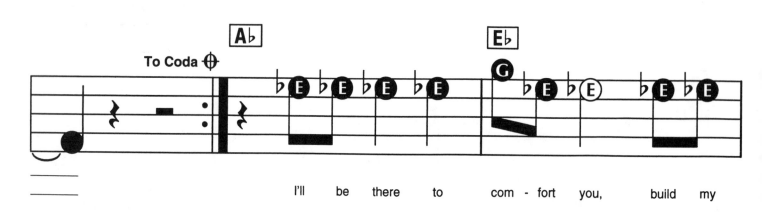

To Coda ⊕

I'll be there to com - fort you, build my

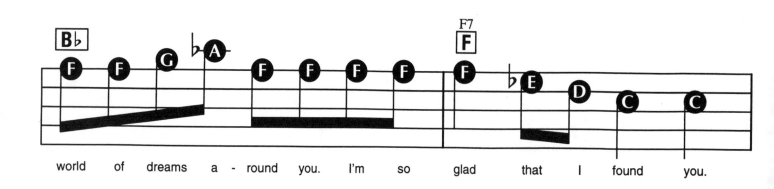

world of dreams a - round you. I'm so glad that I found you.

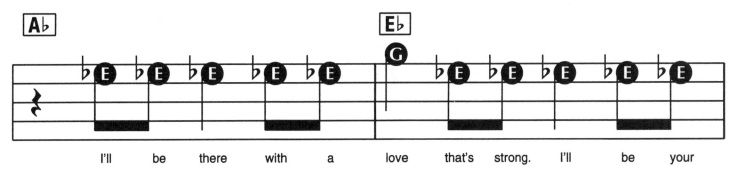

I'll be there with a love that's strong. I'll be your

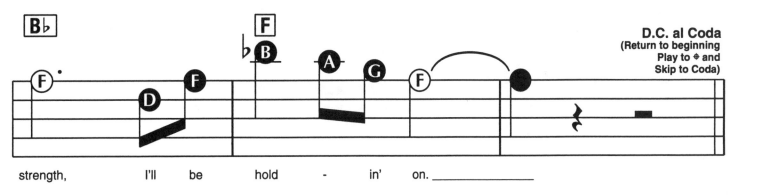

D.C. al Coda
(Return to beginning
Play to ⊕ and
Skip to Coda)

strength, I'll be hold - in' on. _____

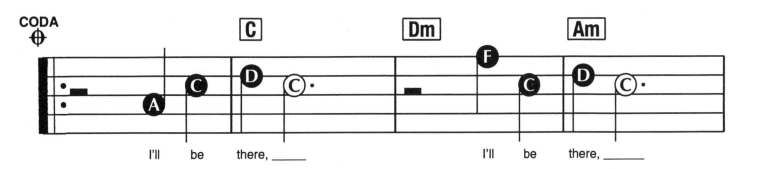

I'll be there, _____ I'll be there, _____

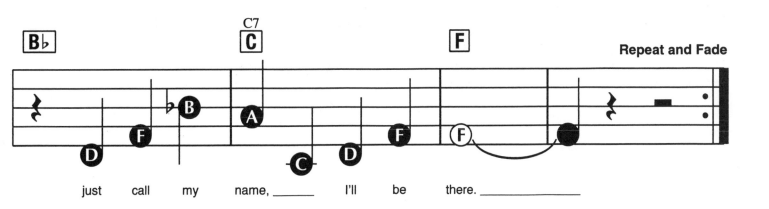

Repeat and Fade

just call my name, _____ I'll be there. _____

Additional Lyrics

3. Let me fill your heart with joy and laughter.
   Togetherness, girl, is all I'm after.
   Whenever you need me, I'll be there.

4. I'll be there to protect you
   With unselfish love that respects you.
   Just call my name, I'll be there.

I've Grown Accustomed to Her Face

from MY FAIR LADY

Registration 7
Rhythm: 8 Beat or Pops

Words by Alan Jay Lerner
Music by Frederick Loewe

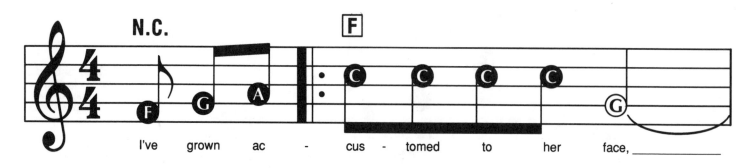

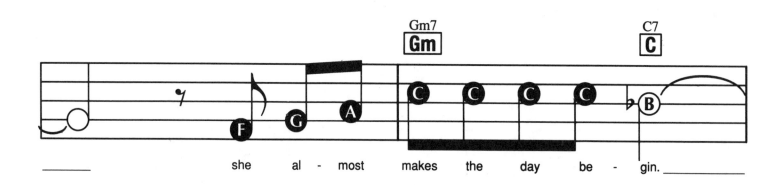

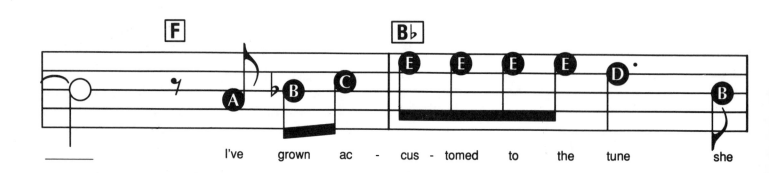

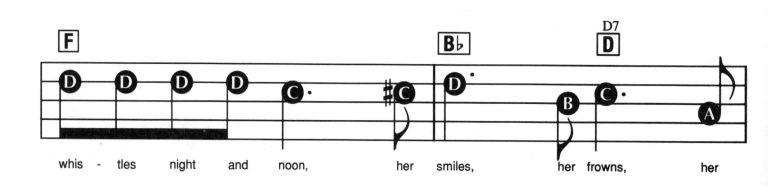

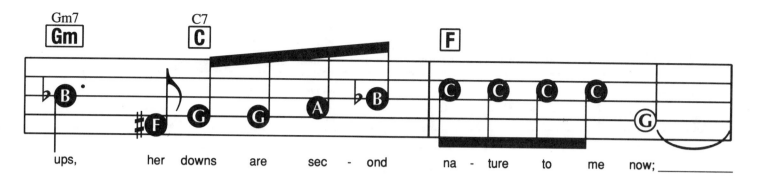

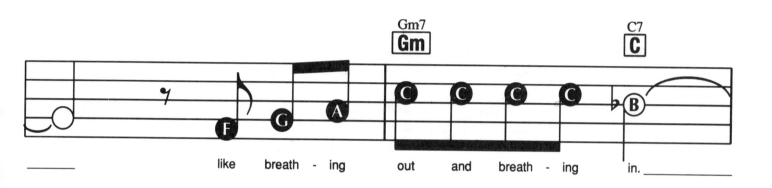

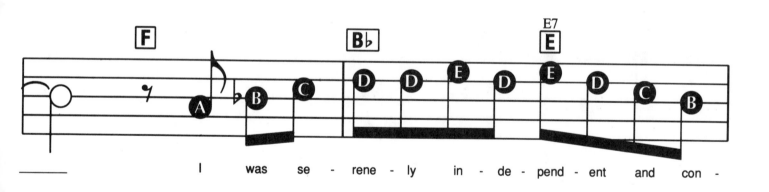

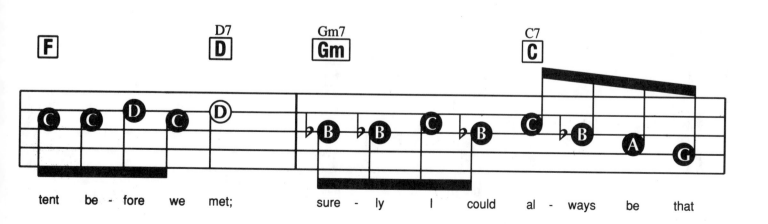

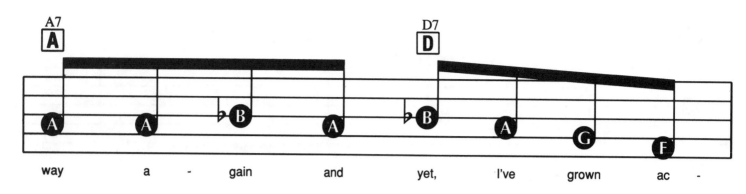

way a - gain and yet, I've grown ac -

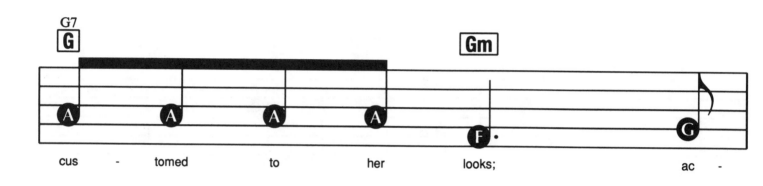

cus - tomed to her looks; ac -

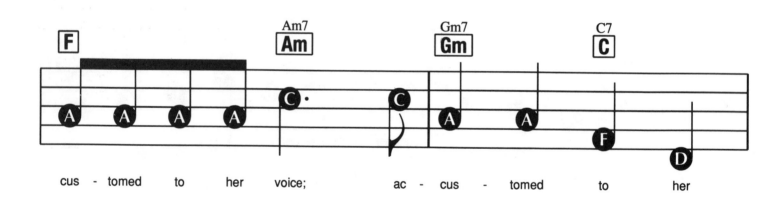

cus - tomed to her voice; ac - cus - tomed to her

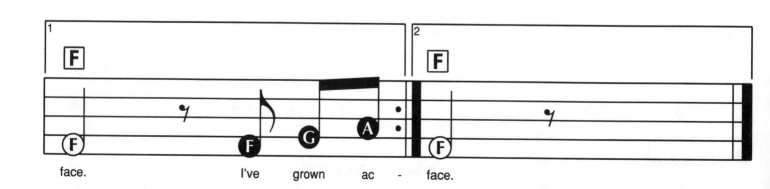

face. I've grown ac - face.

It's Impossible
(Somos novios)

Registration 4
Rhythm: Rhumba or Latin

English Lyric by Sid Wayne
Spanish Words and Music by
Armando Manzanero

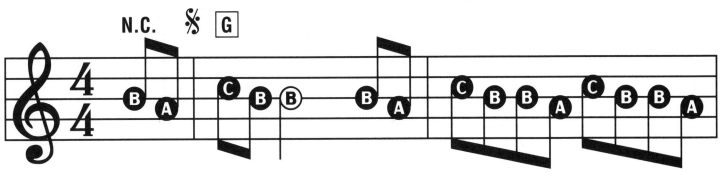

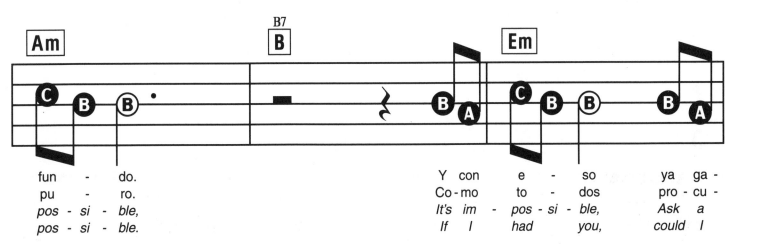

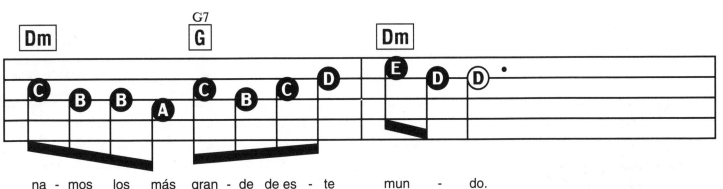

74

CODA

dar - nos el más dul - ce de los be - sos re - cor -
ask me for the world, some - how I'd get it, I would

dar de que co - lor son los ce - re - zos sin ha - cer más co - men - ta - rios so - mos
sell my ver - y soul and not re - gret it, For to live with - out your love is just im -

no - vios so - mos no - vios
pos - si - ble, im - pos - si - ble.

siem - pre no - vios. _____
Mm, _____ im - pos - si - ble. _____

If

Registration 2
Rhythm: Slow Rock or Ballad

Words and Music by
David Gates

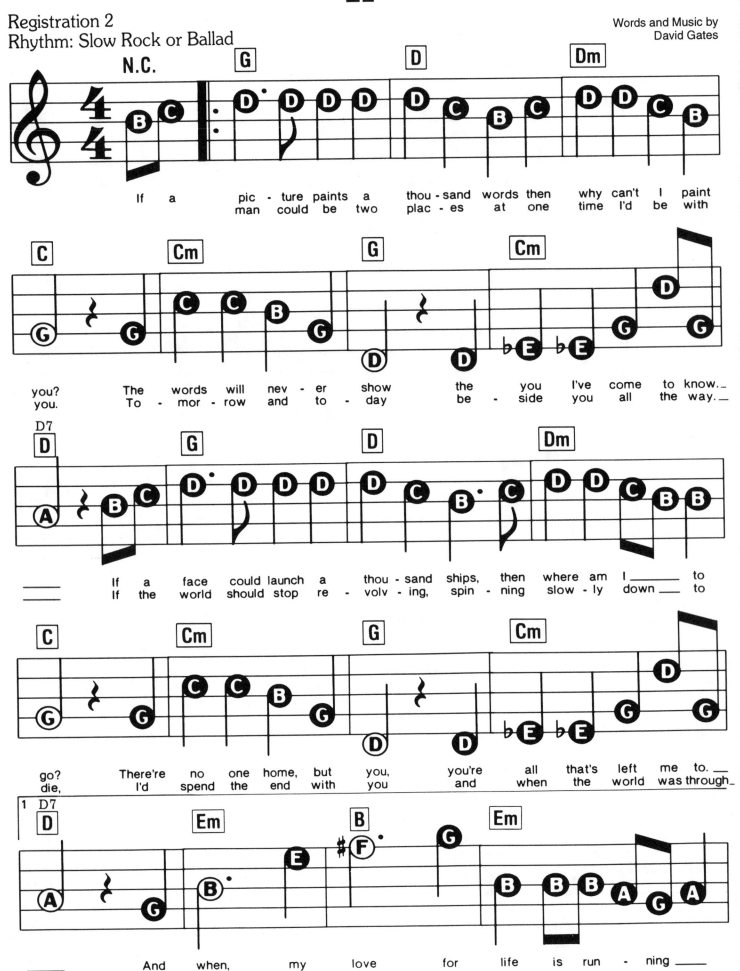

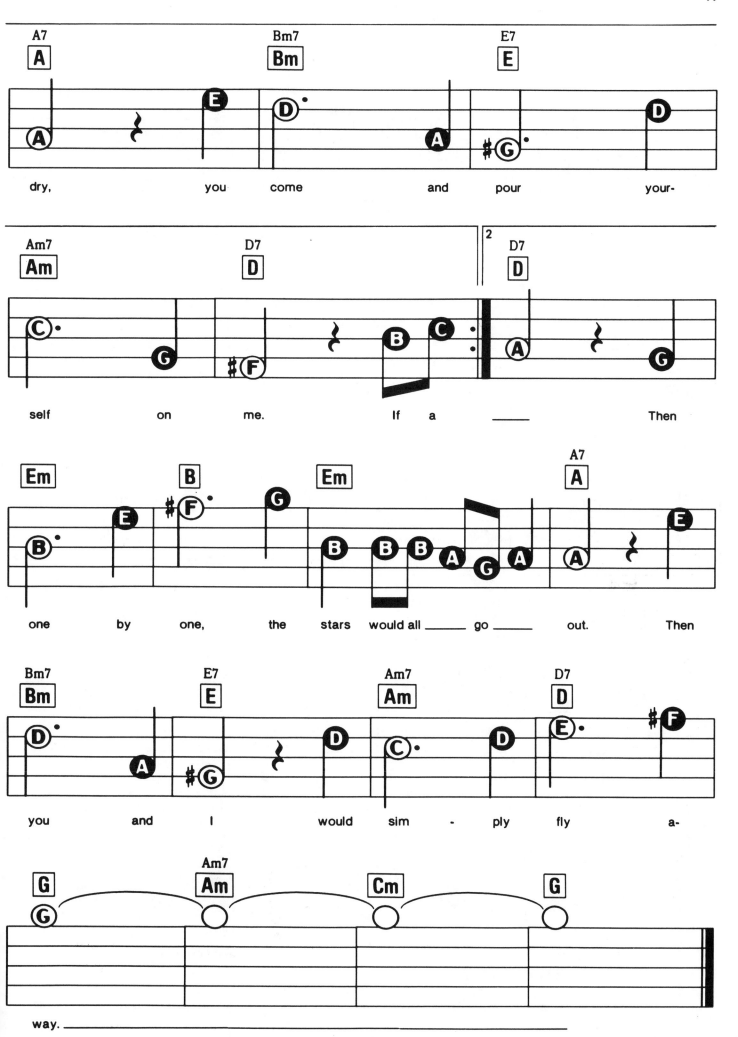

In My Life

Registration 2
Rhythm: 8 Beat or Rock

Words and Music by John Lennon
and Paul McCartney

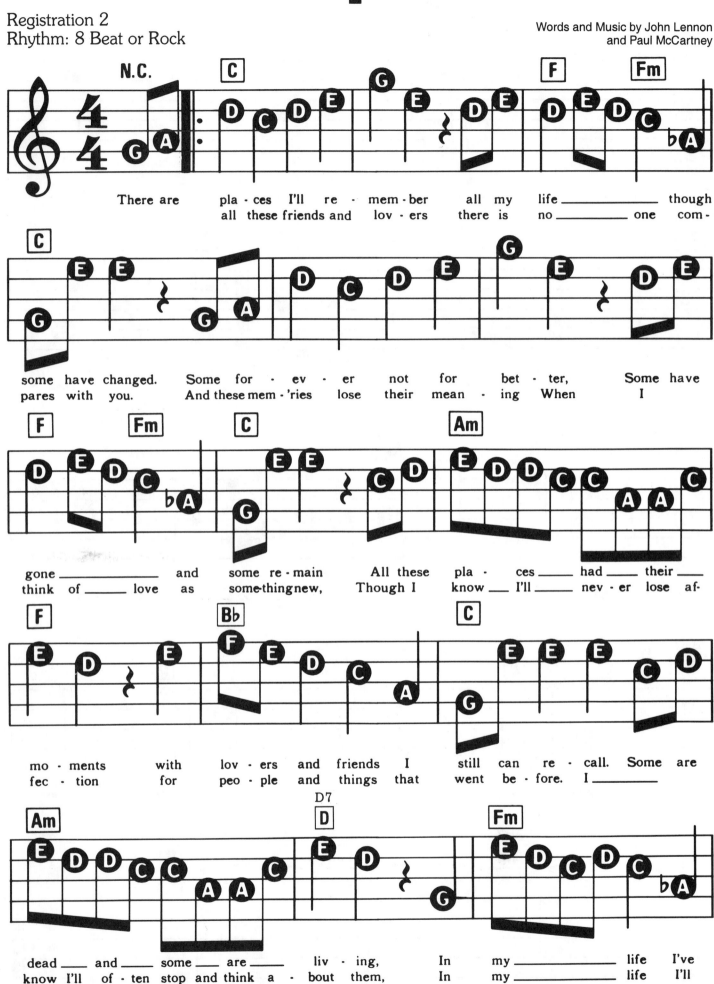

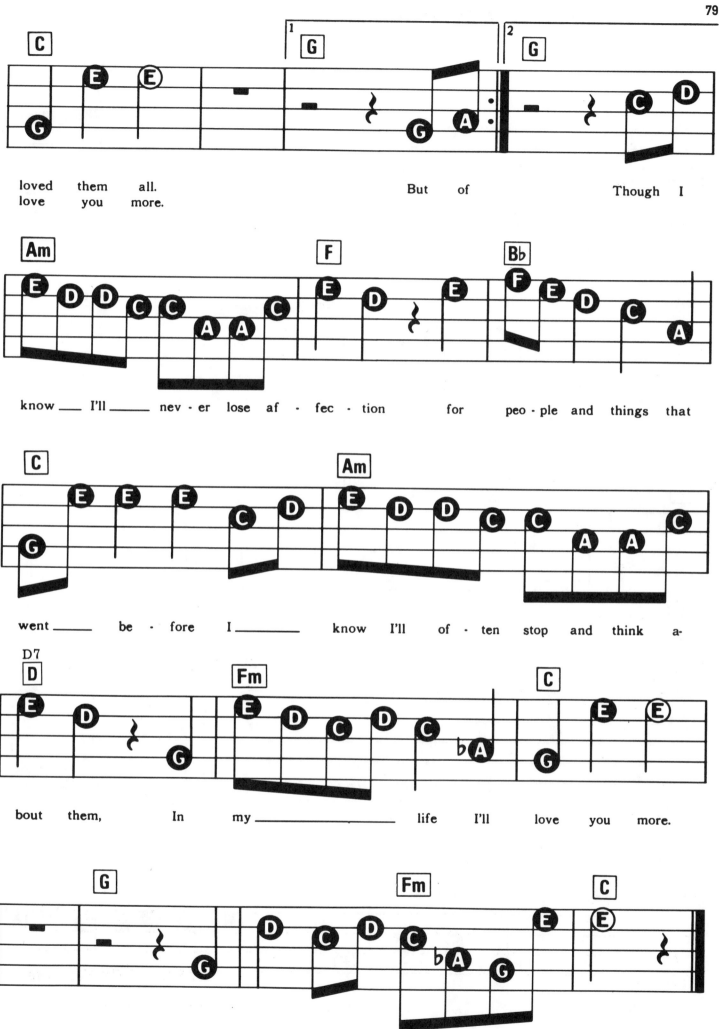

loved them all.
love you more.
But of
Though I

know ___ I'll ___ nev-er lose af-fec-tion for peo-ple and things that

went ___ be-fore I ___ know I'll of-ten stop and think a-

bout them, In my _____ life I'll love you more.

In my _____ life I'll love you more.

Just One More Chance

Registration 4
Rhythm: Swing

Words by Sam Coslow
Music by Arthur Johnston

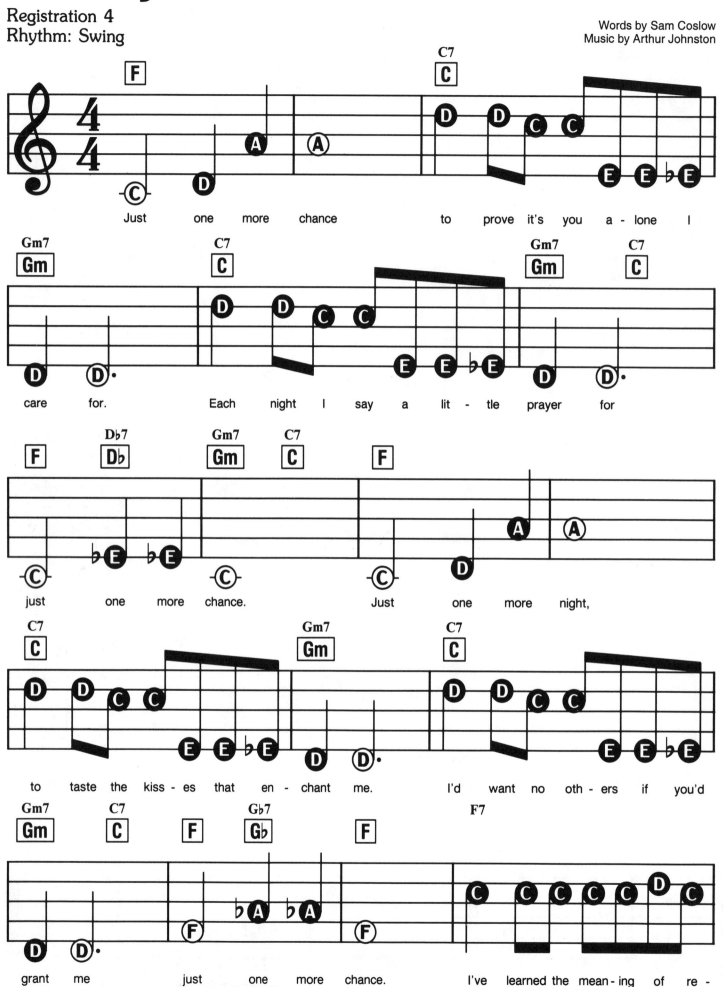

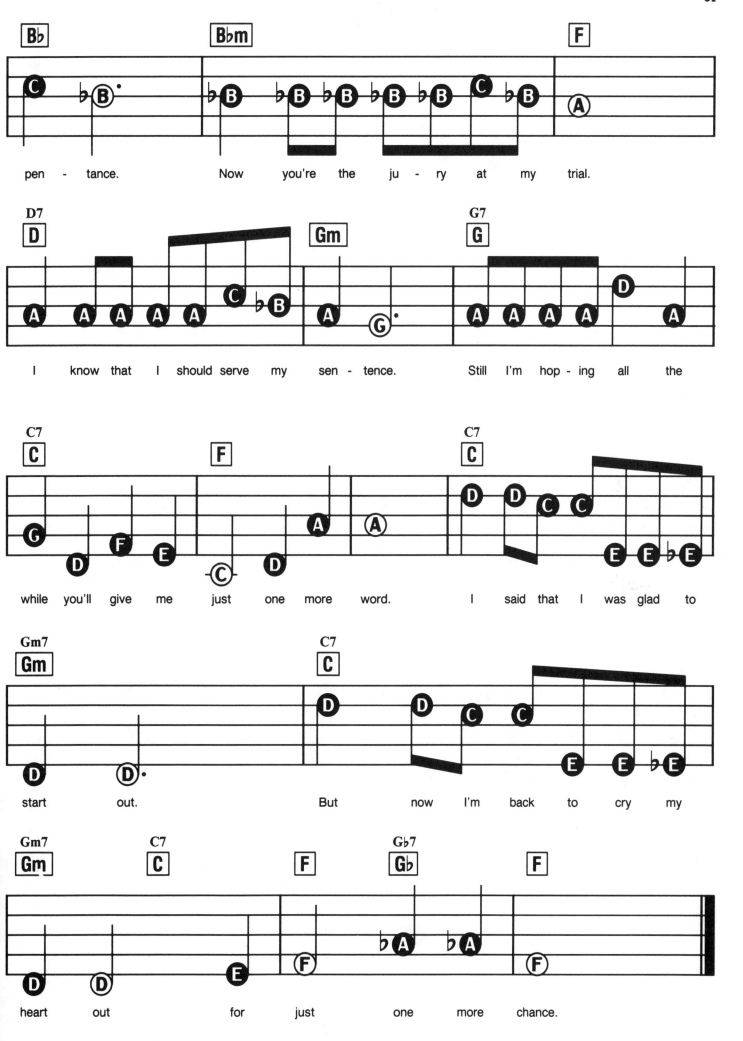

Just the Way You Are

Registration 4
Rhythm: Rock or Jazz Rock

Words and Music by
Billy Joel

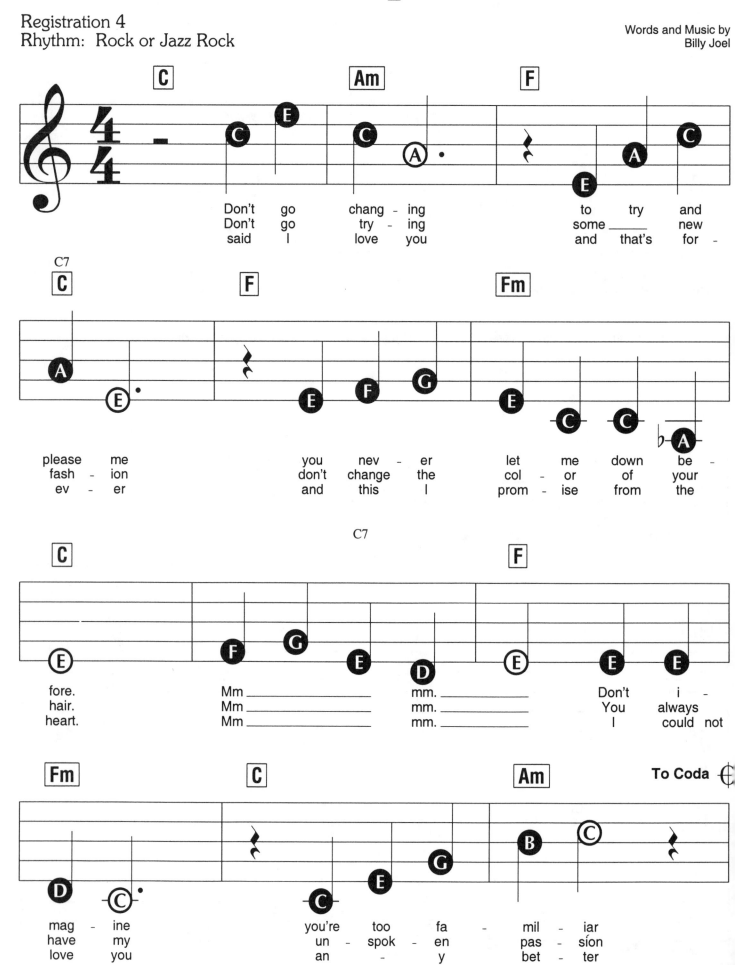

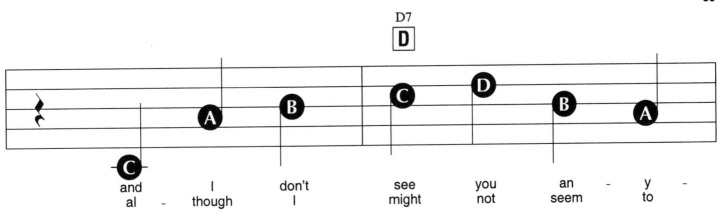

and   I   don't   see   you   an   -   y   -
al   -   though   I   might   you   not   seem   to

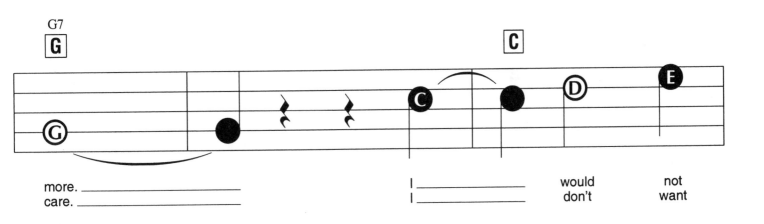

more. _____   I _____   would   not
care. _____   I _____   don't   want

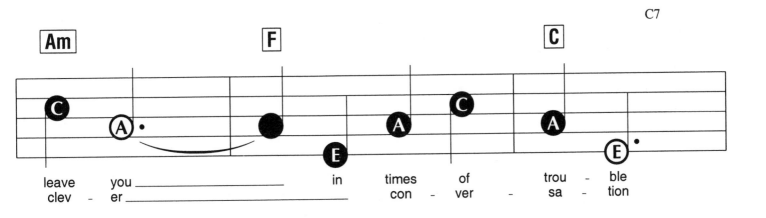

leave   you _____   in   times   of   trou   -   ble
clev   -   er _____   con   -   ver   -   sa   -   tion

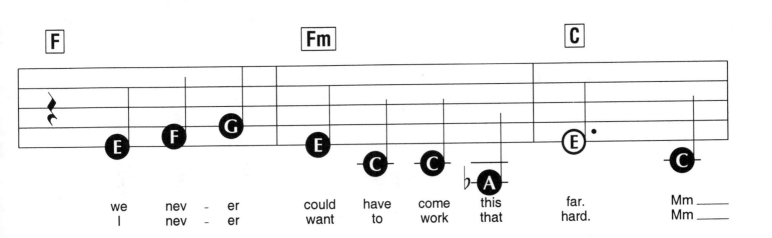

we   nev   -   er   could   have   come   this   far.   Mm ___
I   nev   -   er   want   to   work   that   hard.   Mm ___

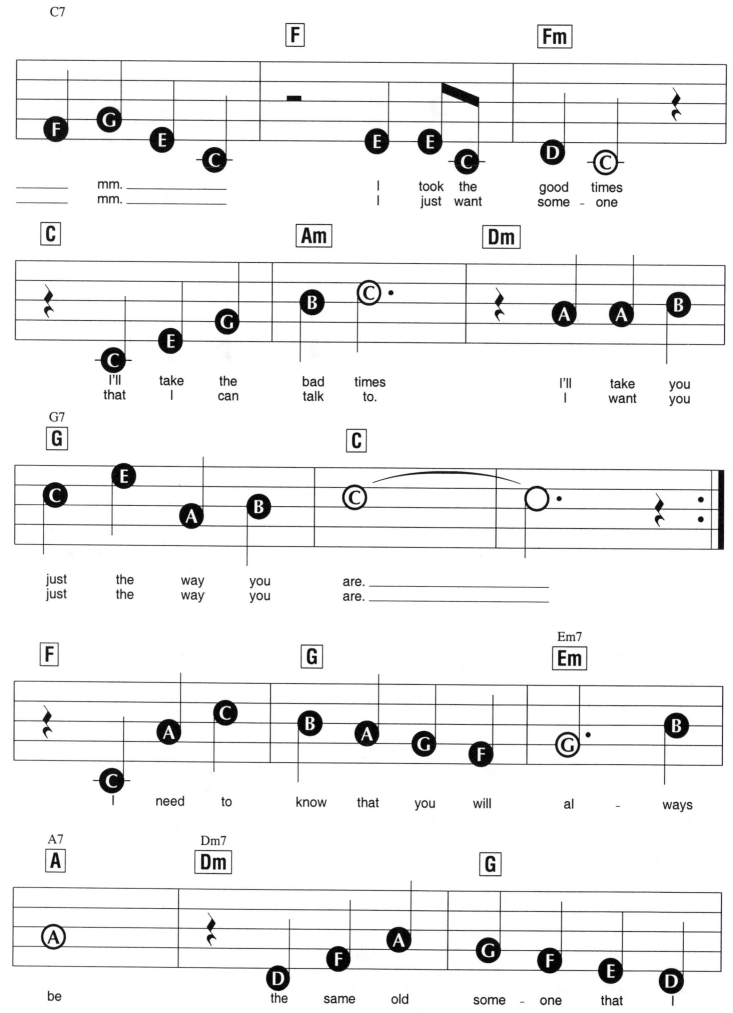

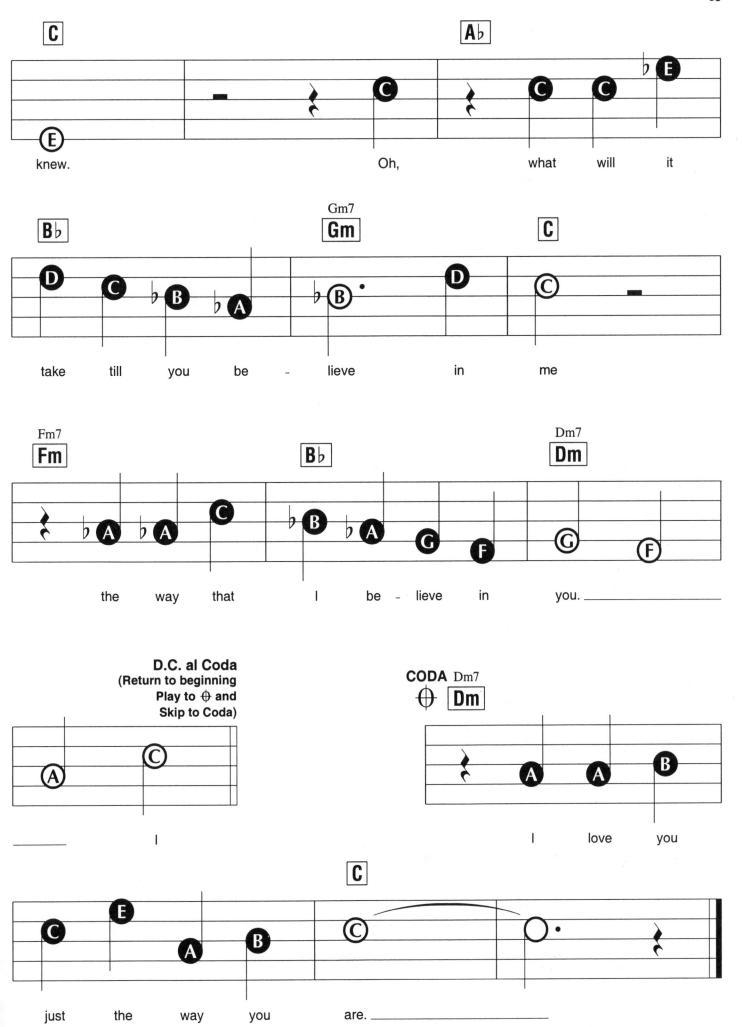

Make It with You

Registration 1
Rhythm: Ballad

Words and Music by
David Gates

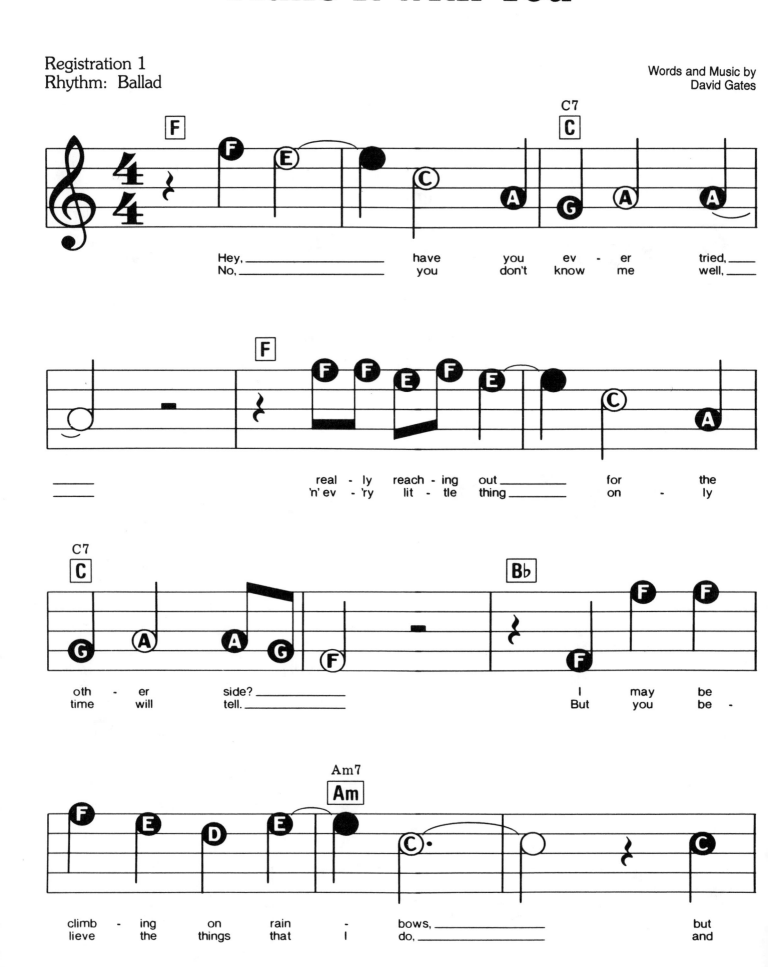

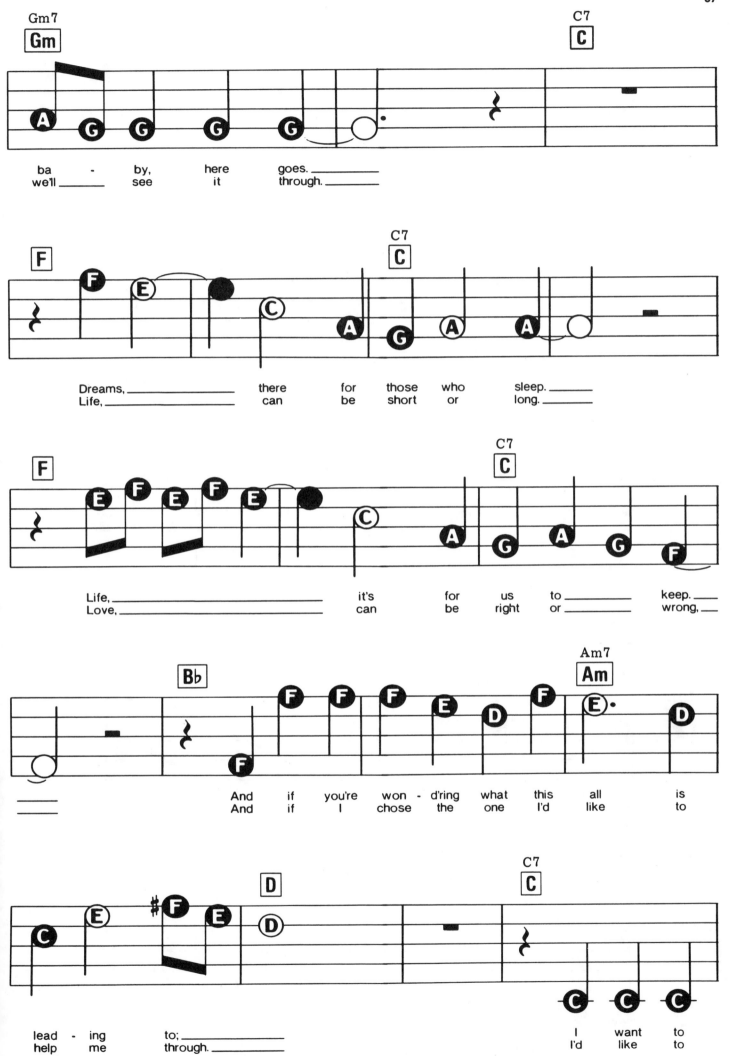

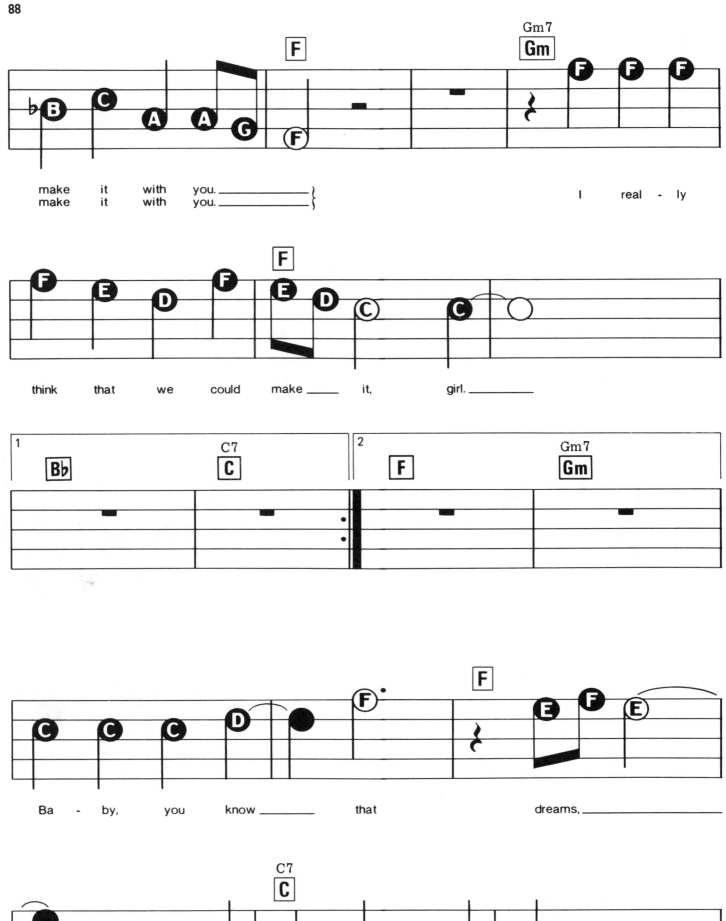

make it with you. _____
make it with you. _____   I real - ly

think that we could make ___ it, girl. _____

Ba - by, you know _____ that dreams, _____

_____ they're for those who sleep. _____

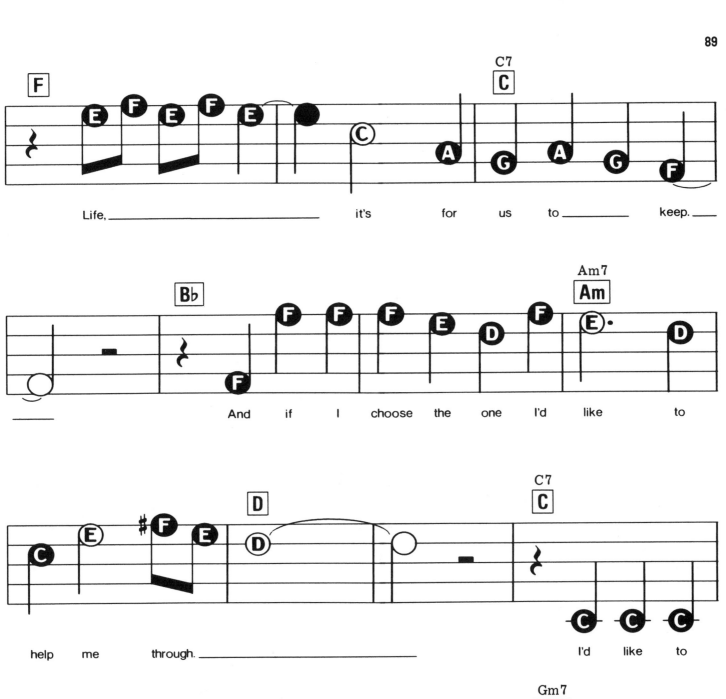

Life,_____ it's for us to _____ keep. ____

_____ And if I choose the one I'd like to

help me through. _____ I'd like to

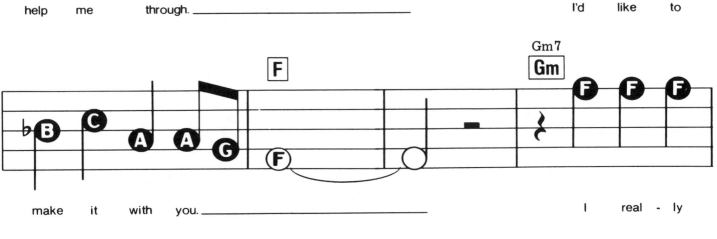

make it with you. _____ I real - ly

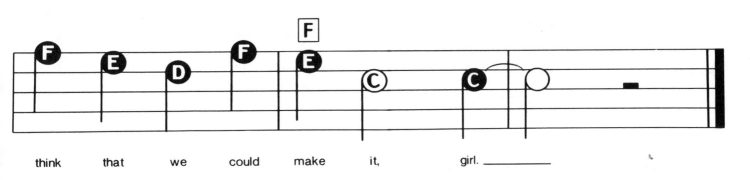

think that we could make it, girl. _____

More Than You Know

Registration 8
Rhythm: Fox Trot

Words by William Rose and Edward Eliscu
Music by Vincent Youmans

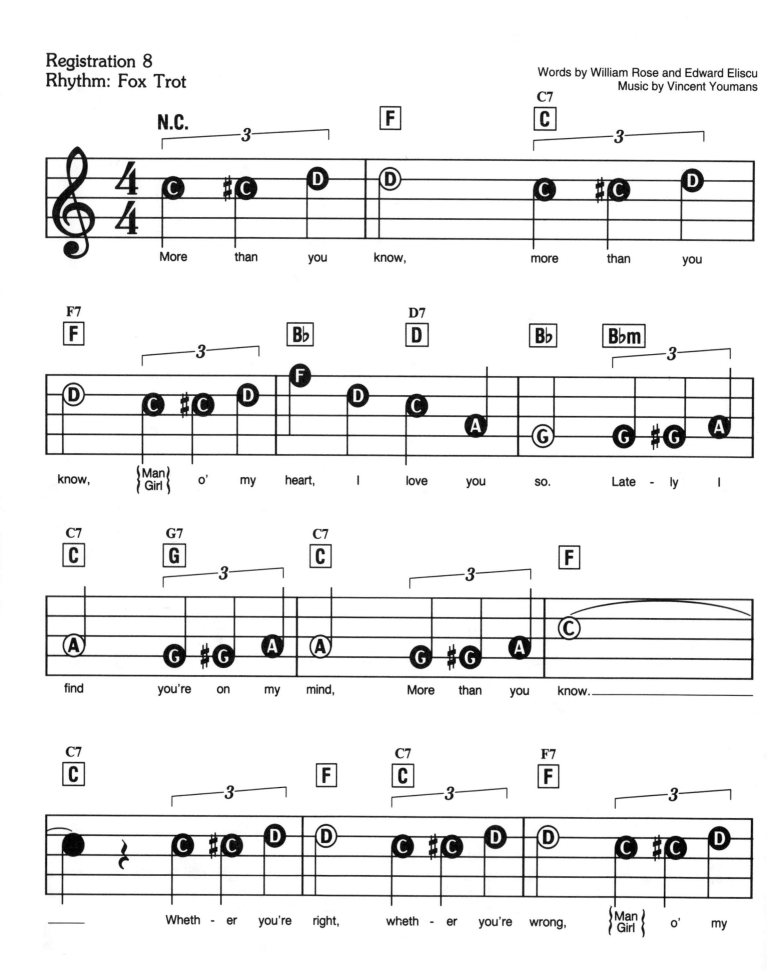

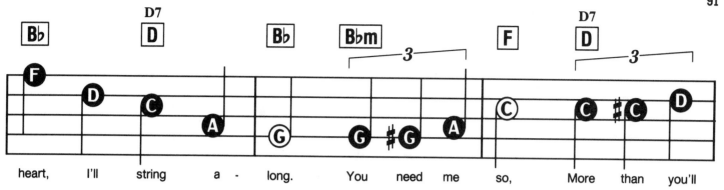

heart, I'll string a - long. You need me so, More than you'll

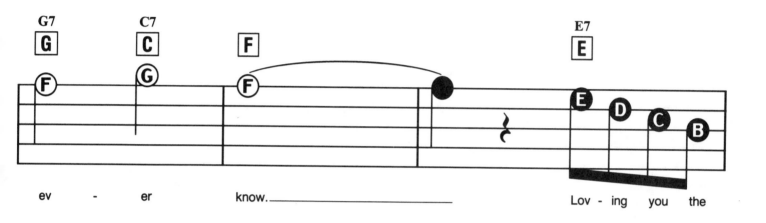

ev - er know. Lov - ing you the

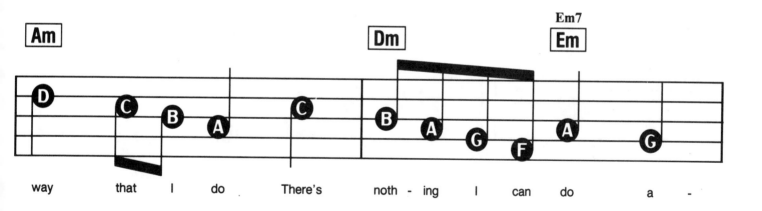

way that I do There's noth - ing I can do a -

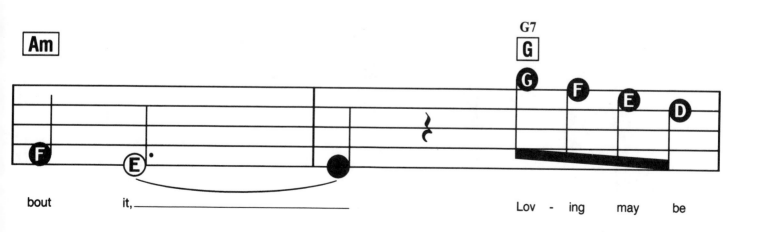

bout it, Lov - ing may be

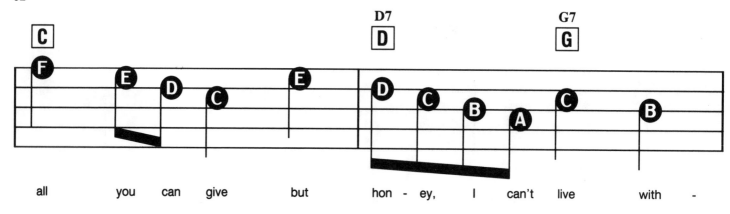

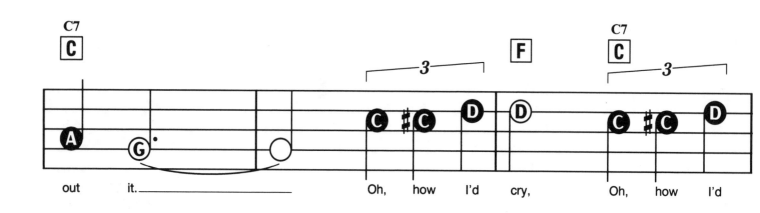

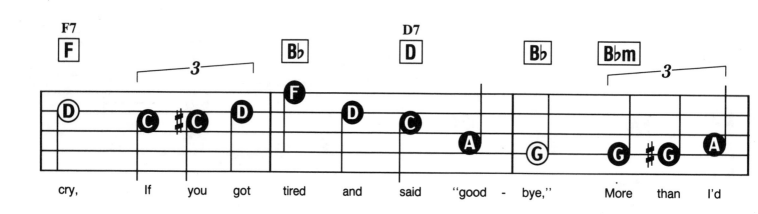

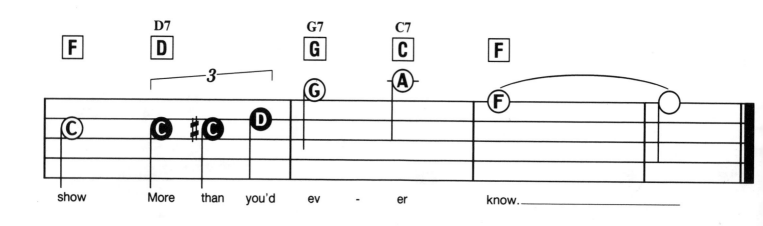

My Foolish Heart

Registration 9
Rhythm: Ballad

Words by Ned Washington
Music by Victor Young

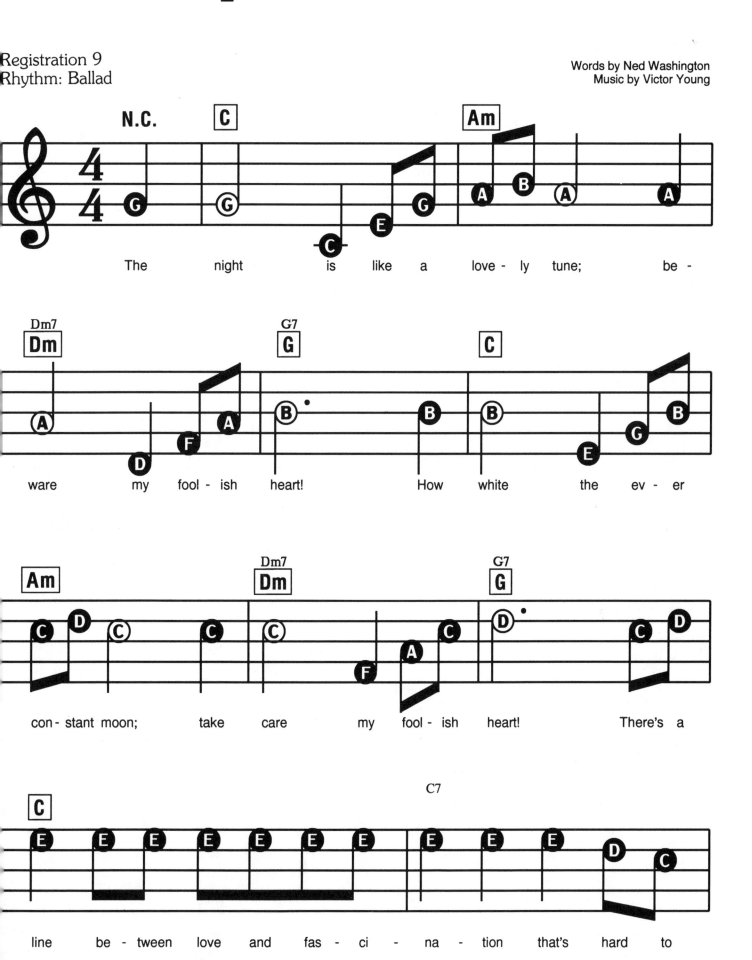

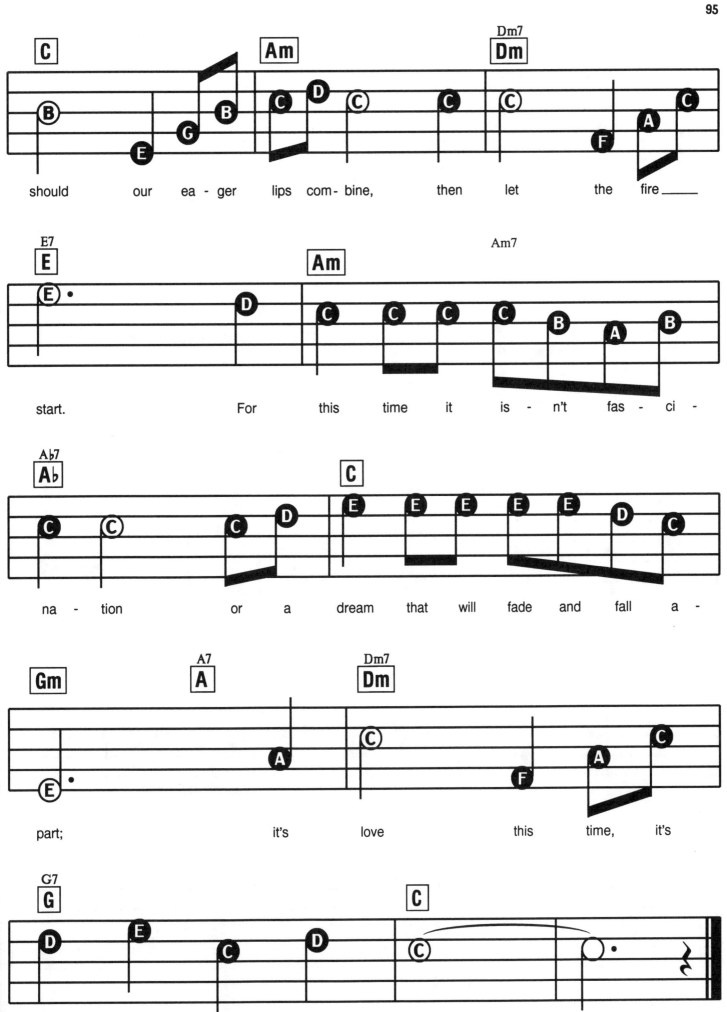

My Cherie Amour

Registration 7
Rhythm: Rock or Bossa Nova

Words and Music by Stevie Wonder,
Sylvia Moy and Henry Cosby

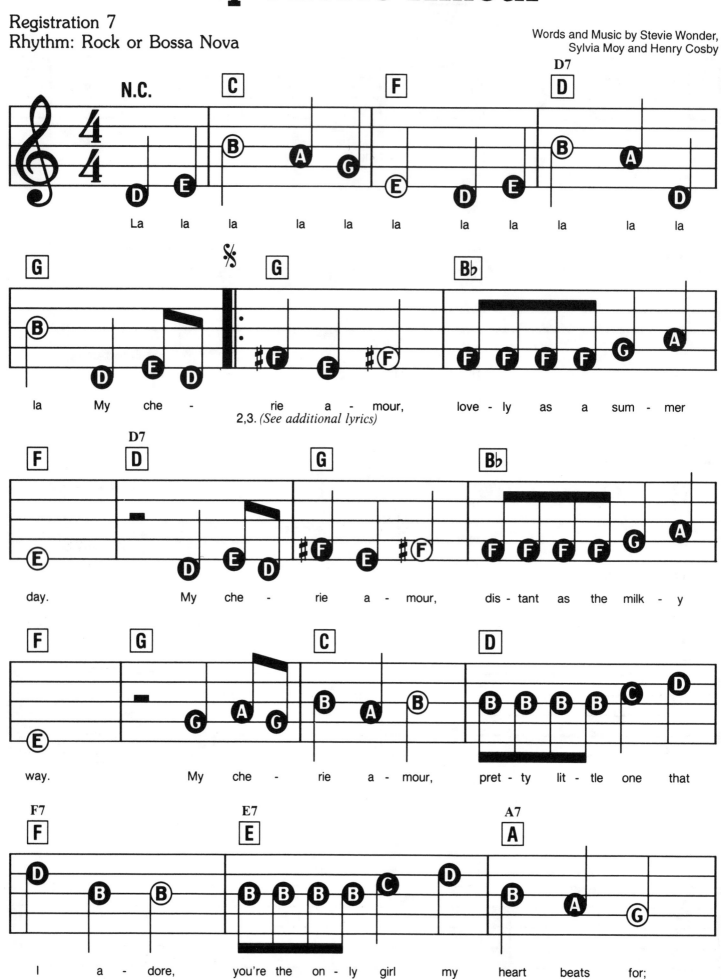

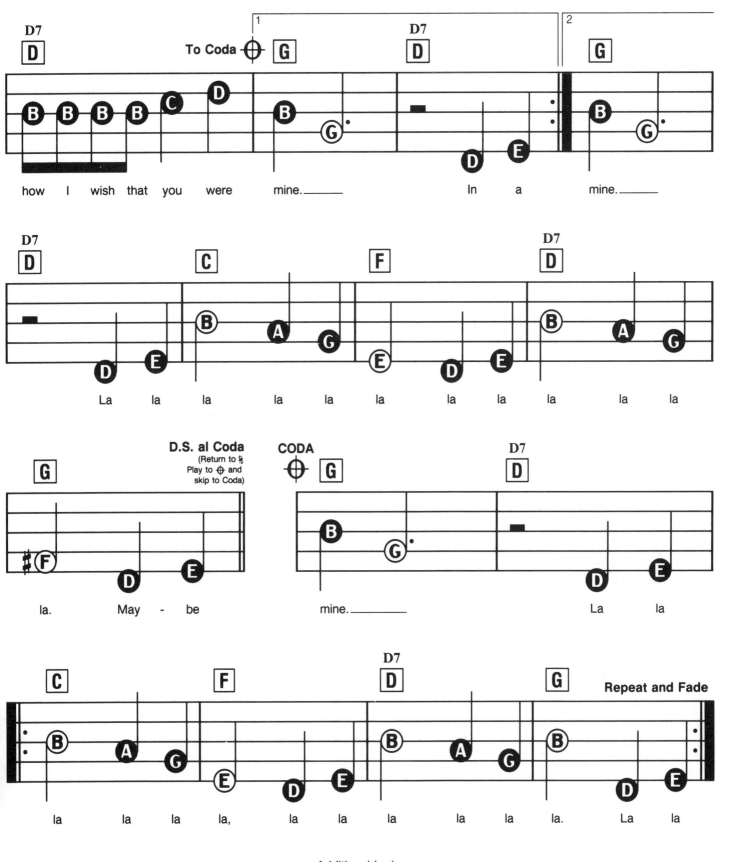

Additional Lyrics

2. In a cafe, or sometimes on a crowded street,
   I've been near you, but you never notice me.
   My cherie amour, won't you tell me how could you ignore,
   That behind that little smile I wore, how I wish that you were mine.

3. Maybe someday you'll see my face among the crowd;
   Maybe someday I'll share your little distant cloud.
   Oh, cherie amour, pretty little one that I adore,
   You're the only girl my heart beats for; how I wish that you were mine.

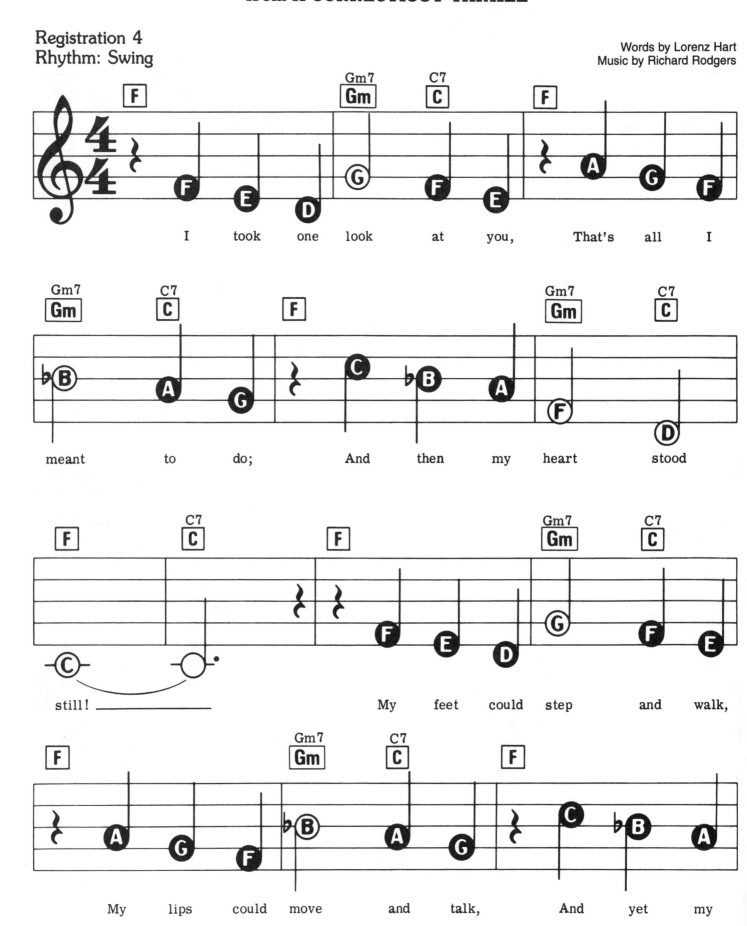

My Heart Stood Still
from A CONNECTICUT YANKEE

Registration 4
Rhythm: Swing

Words by Lorenz Hart
Music by Richard Rodgers

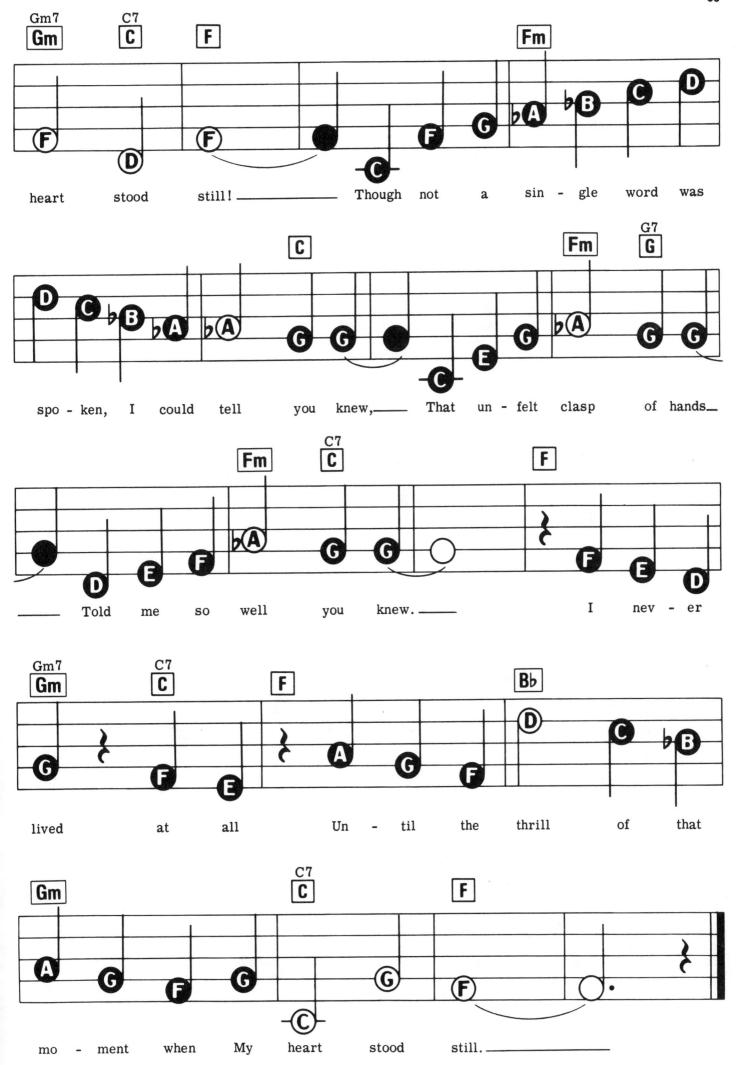

(You Make Me Feel Like)
A Natural Woman

Registration 7
Rhythm: Waltz or Slow Rock

Words and Music by Gerry Goffin,
Carole King and Jerry Wexler

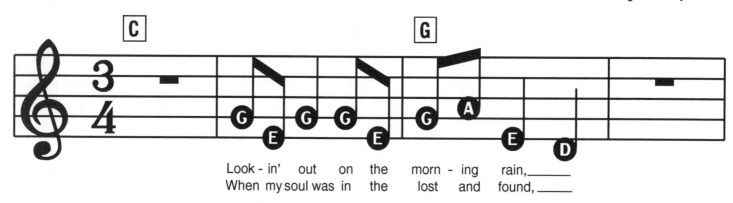

Look - in' out on the morn - ing rain,_____
When my soul was in the lost and found, _____

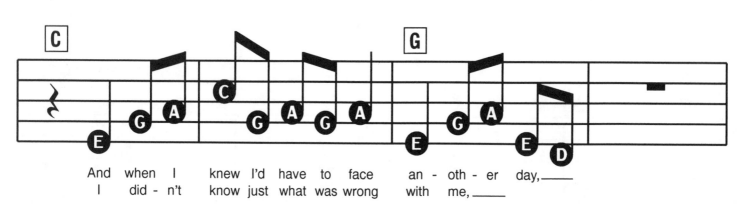

I used to feel un - in - spired. _____
you came a - long to claim it.

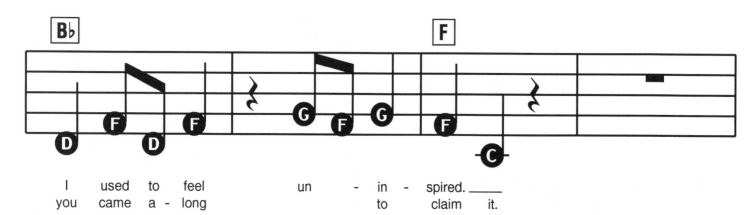

And when I knew I'd have to face an - oth - er day,_____
I did - n't know just what was wrong with me, _____

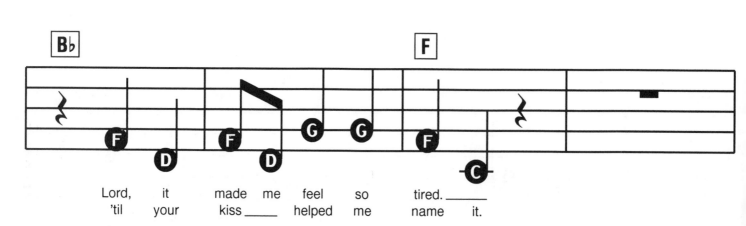

Lord, it made me feel so tired. _____
'til your kiss _____ helped me name it.

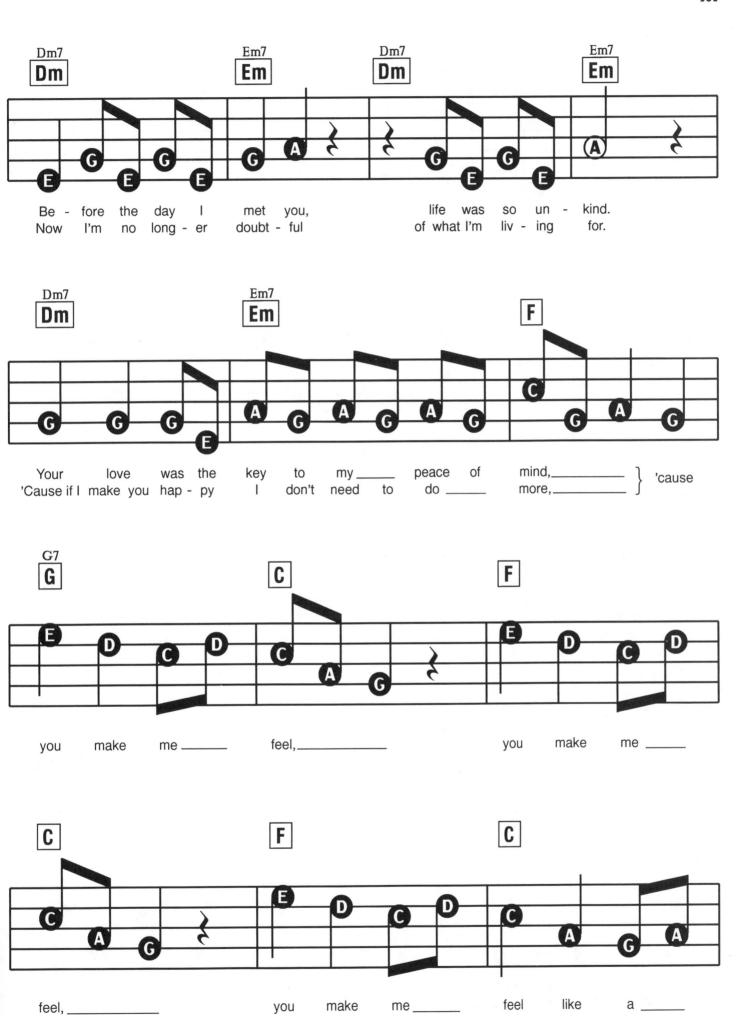

Be - fore the day I met you, life was so un - kind.
Now I'm no long - er doubt - ful of what I'm liv - ing for.

Your love was the key to my____ peace of mind,_____ } 'cause
'Cause if I make you hap - py I don't need to do _____ more,_____

you make me _____ feel,_____ you make me _____

feel, _____ you make me _____ feel like a _____

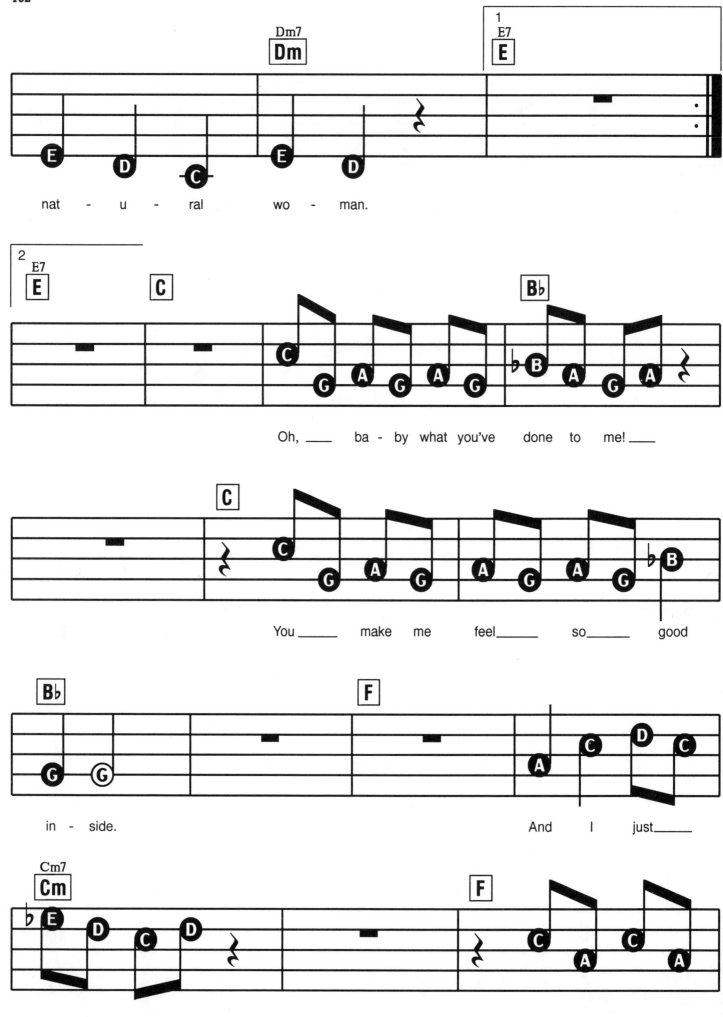

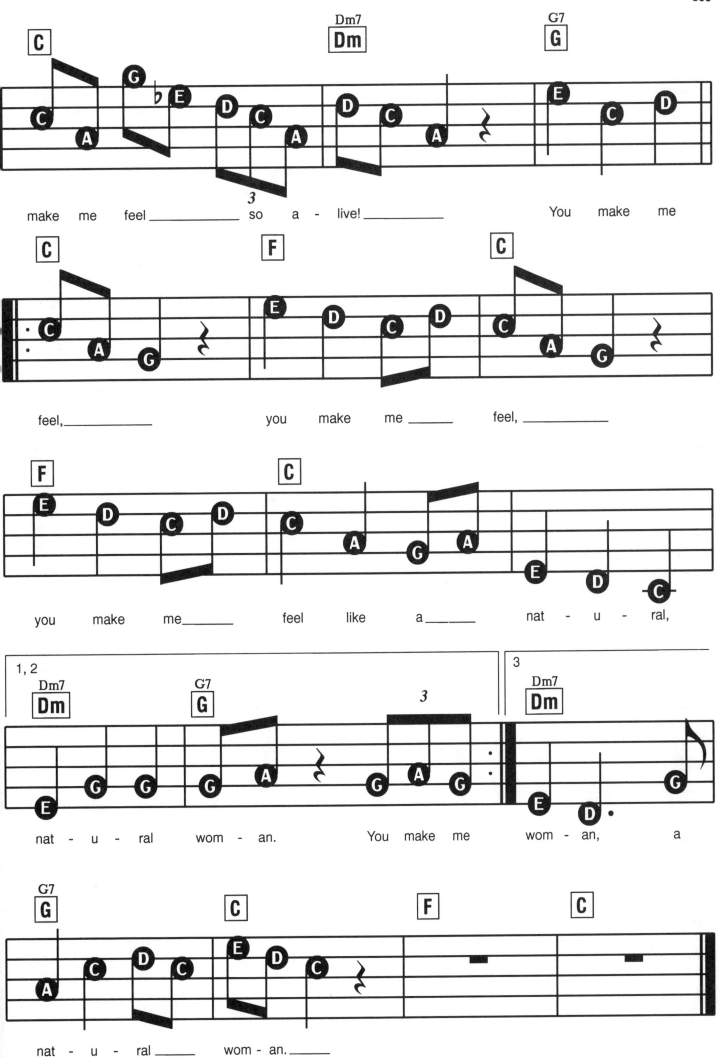

The Nearness of You
from the Paramount Picture ROMANCE IN THE DARK

Registration 9
Rhythm: Fox Trot or Swing

Words by Ned Washington
Music by Hoagy Carmichael

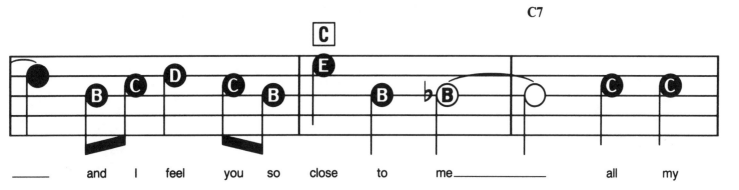

and I feel you so close to me_____ all my

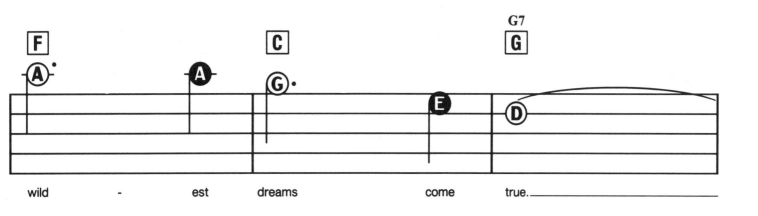

wild - est dreams come true._____

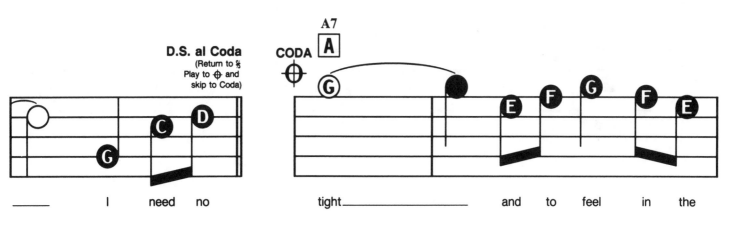

D.S. al Coda
(Return to 𝄋
Play to ⊕ and
skip to Coda)

CODA

_____ I need no tight_____ and to feel in the

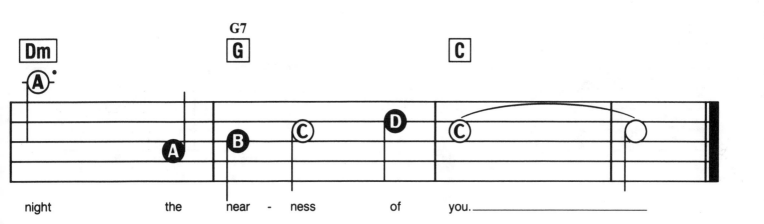

night the near - ness of you._____

Nobody Loves Me Like You Do

Registration 4
Rhythm: Rock or Shuffle

Words by Pamela Phillips
Music by James P. Dunne

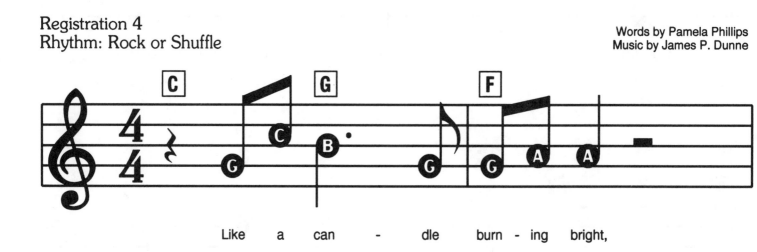

Like a can - dle burn - ing bright,

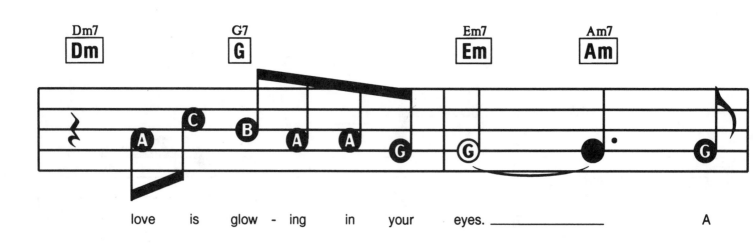

love is glow - ing in your eyes. _____ A

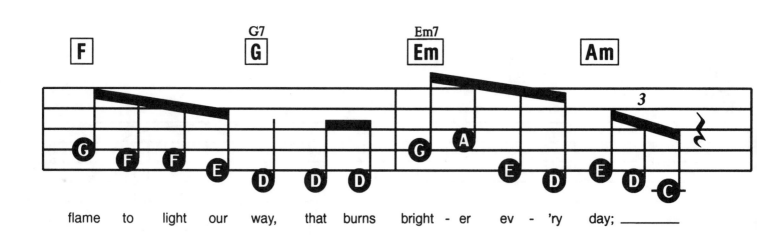

flame to light our way, that burns bright - er ev - 'ry day; _____

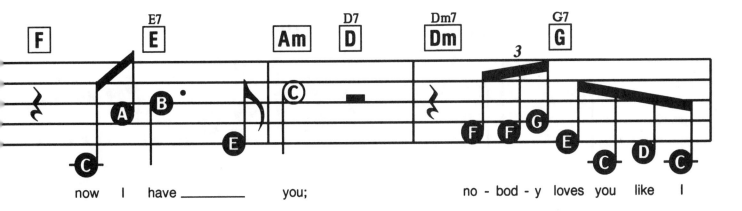

now I have _____ you;   no - bod - y loves you like I

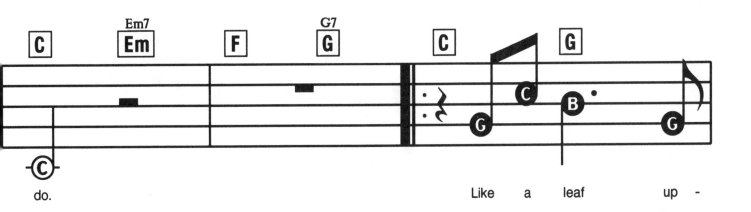

do.   Like a leaf up -

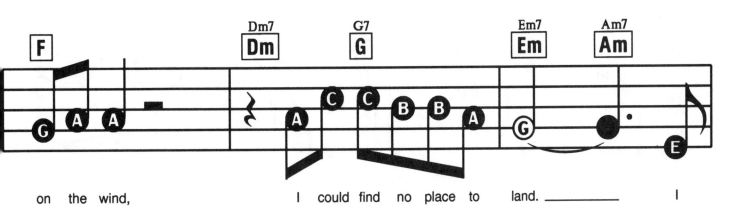

on the wind,   I could find no place to land. _____   I

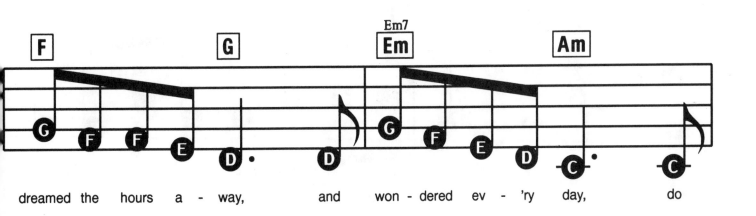

dreamed the hours a - way,   and won - dered ev - 'ry day,   do

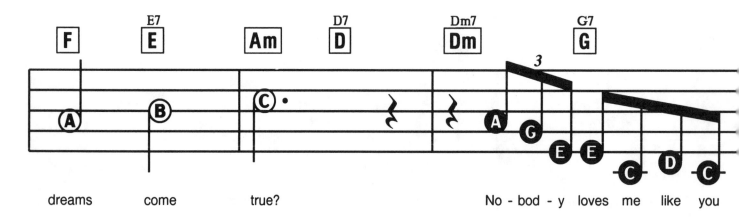

dreams   come   true?   No - bod - y loves me like you

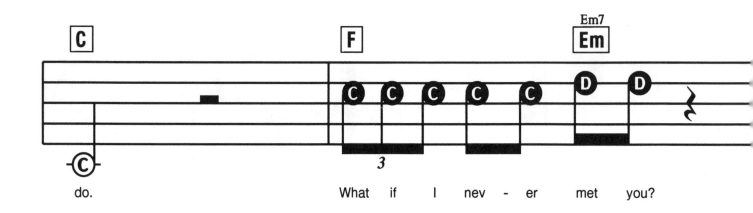

do.   What if I nev - er met you?

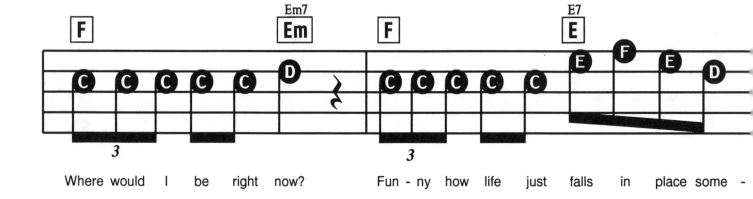

Where would I   be right now?   Fun - ny how life just falls   in place some -

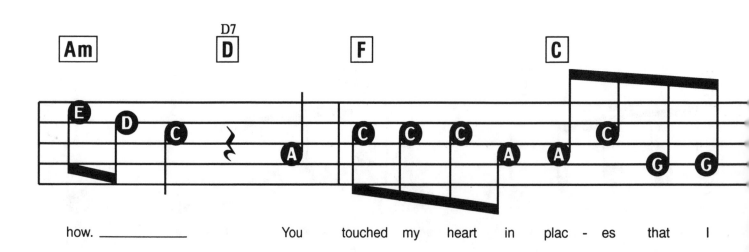

how. _____   You   touched my heart in plac - es that I

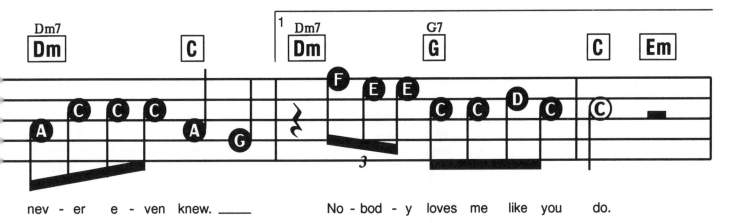

nev - er   e - ven   knew. _____   No - bod - y   loves   me   like   you   do.

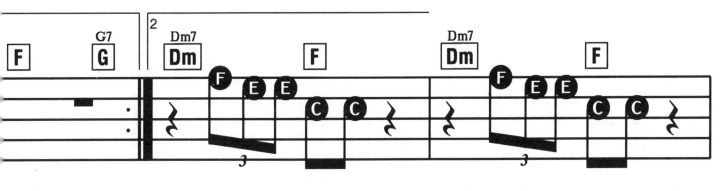

No - bod - y   loves   me,   no - bod - y   loves   me,

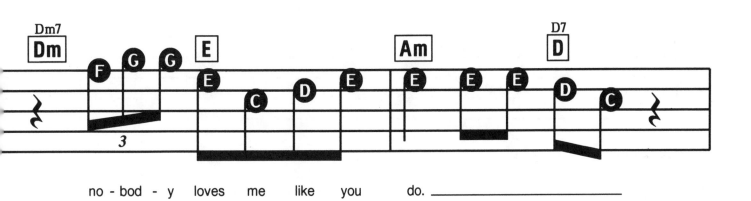

no - bod - y   loves   me   like   you   do. _____

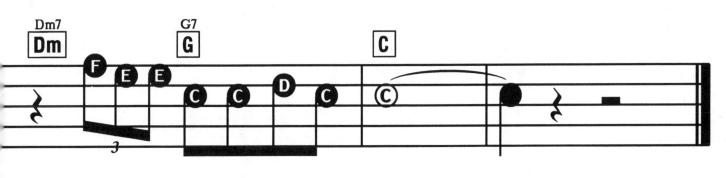

No bod - y   loves   me   like   you   do. _____

Save the Best for Last

Registration 8
Rhythm: 8 Beat

Words and Music by Phil Galdston
Jon Lind and Wendy Waldman

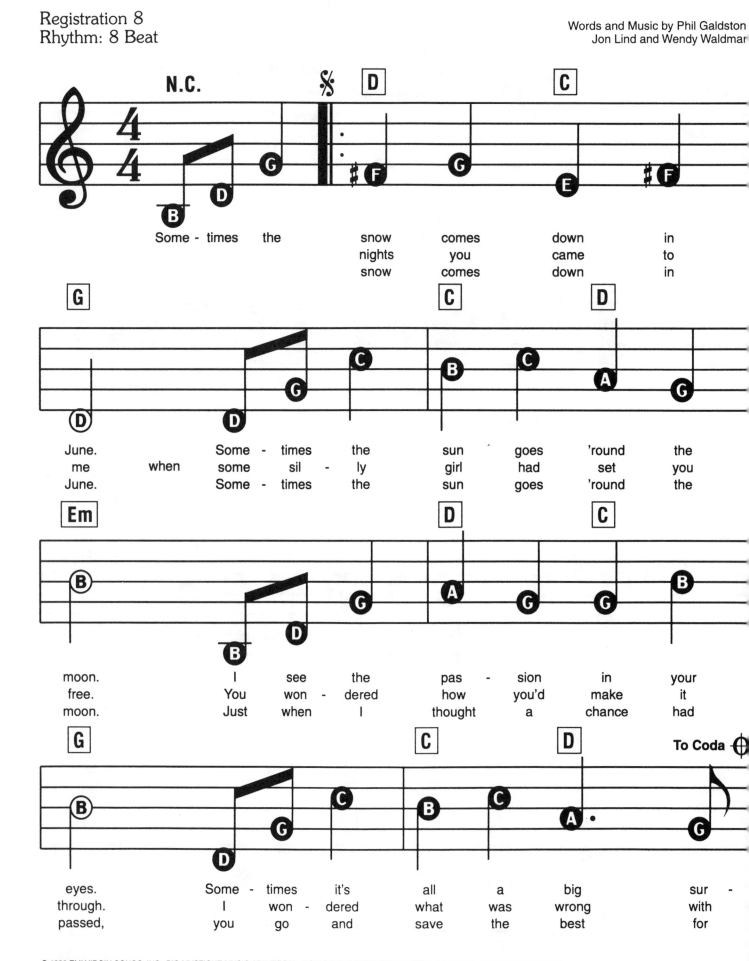

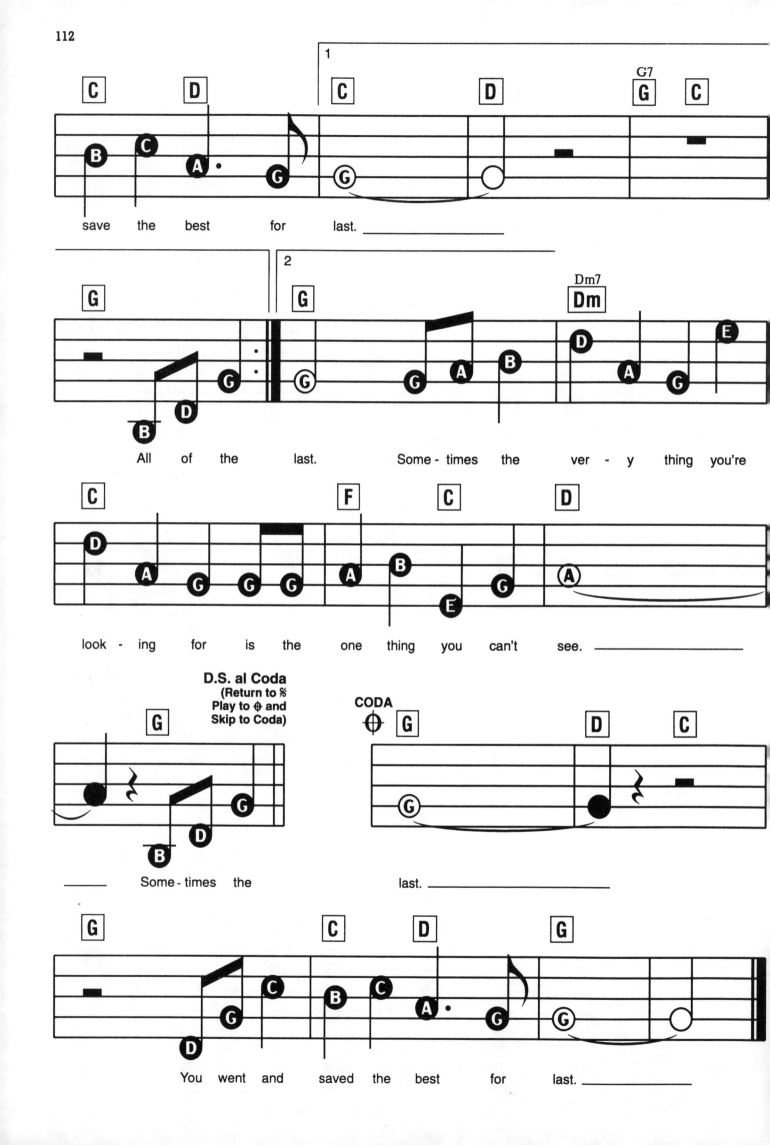

Valentine

Registration 8
Rhythm: Pops or Rock

Words and Music by Jack Kugell
and Jim Brickman

If there were no words, no way to speak,
All of my life, I have been wait - ing for

I would still hear _____ you. If there were no
all you give to _____ me. You've o - pened my

tears, no way to feel in - side, I'd still feel for you. And
eyes and shown me how to love un - self - ish - ly. I've

(1., D.S.) e - ven if the sun re - fused to
(2.) dreamed of this a thou - sand times be -

114

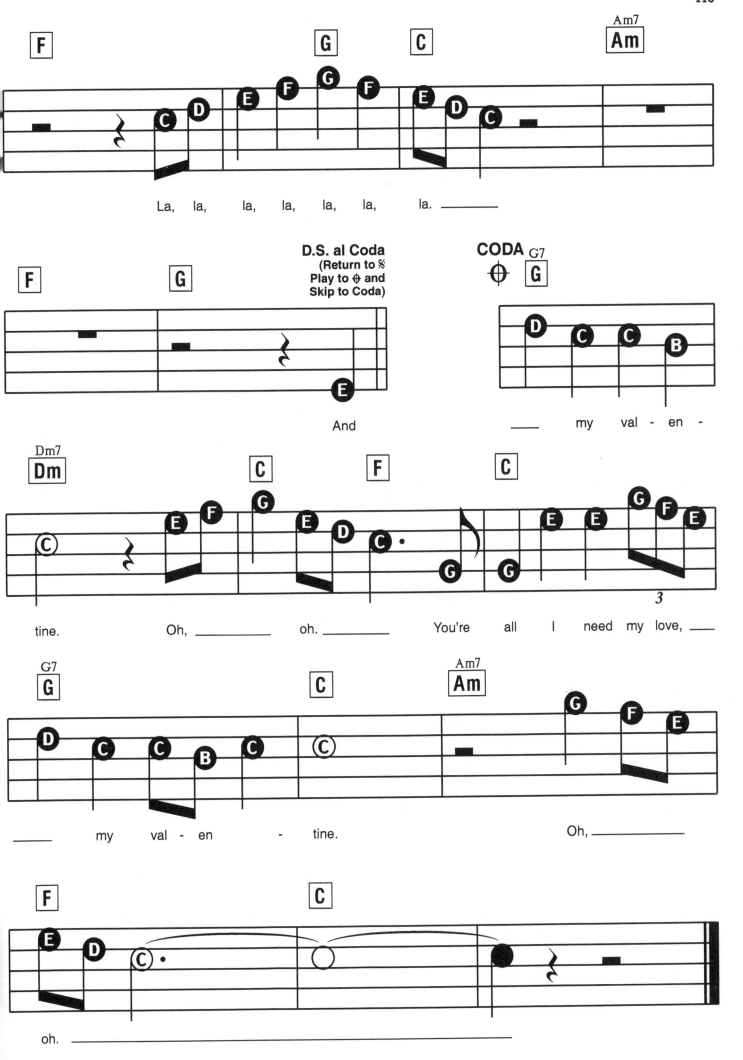

Saving All My Love for You

Registration 1
Rhythm: Rock or Slow Rock

Words by Gerry Goffin
Music by Michael Masser

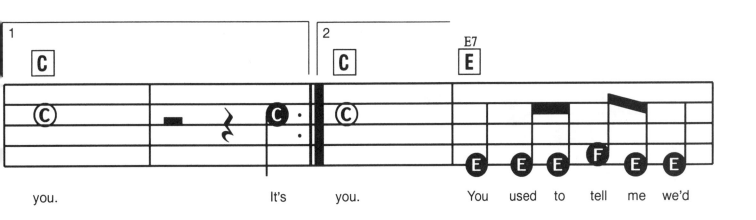

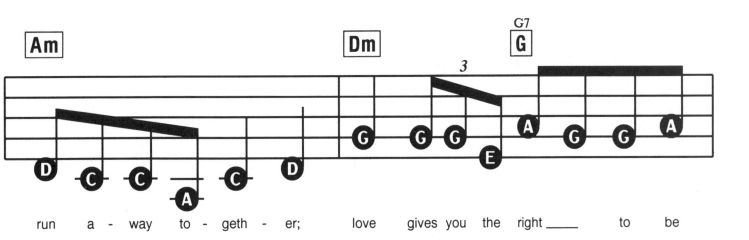

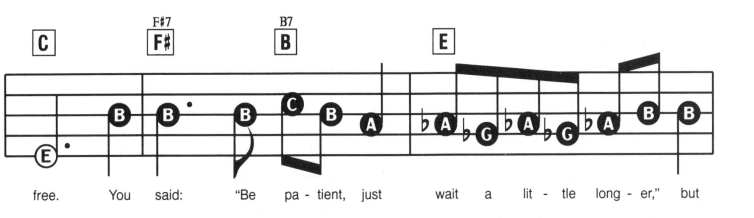

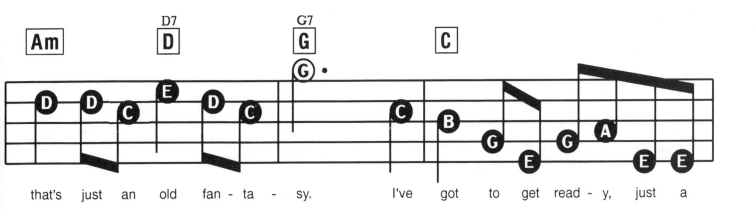

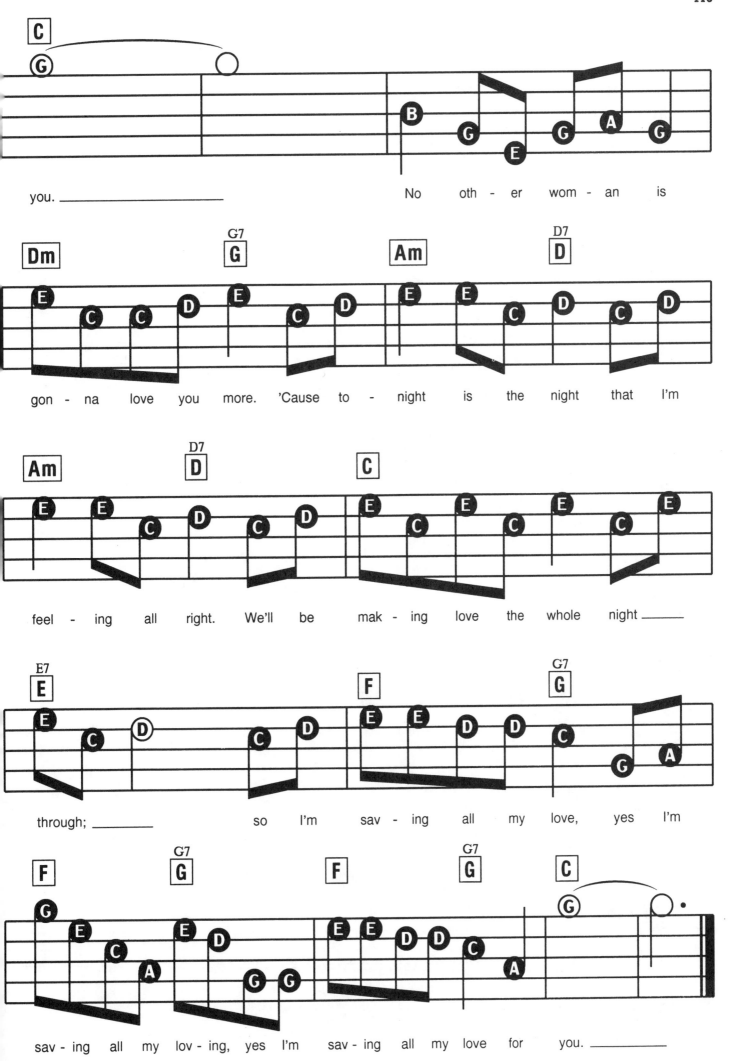

September Song
from the Musical Play KNICKERBOCKER HOLIDAY

Registration 2
Rhythm: Fox Trot

Words by Maxwell Anderson
Music by Kurt Weill

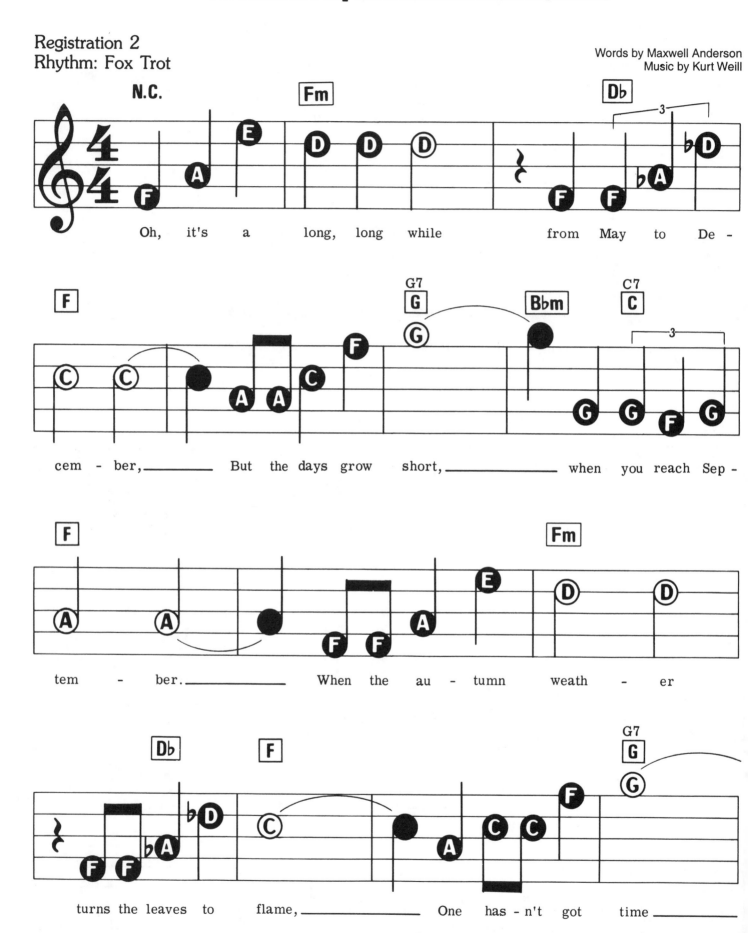

Oh, it's a long, long while from May to De-

cem - ber,_____ But the days grow short,_____ when you reach Sep-

tem - ber._____ When the au - tumn weath - er

turns the leaves to flame,_____ One has - n't got time_____

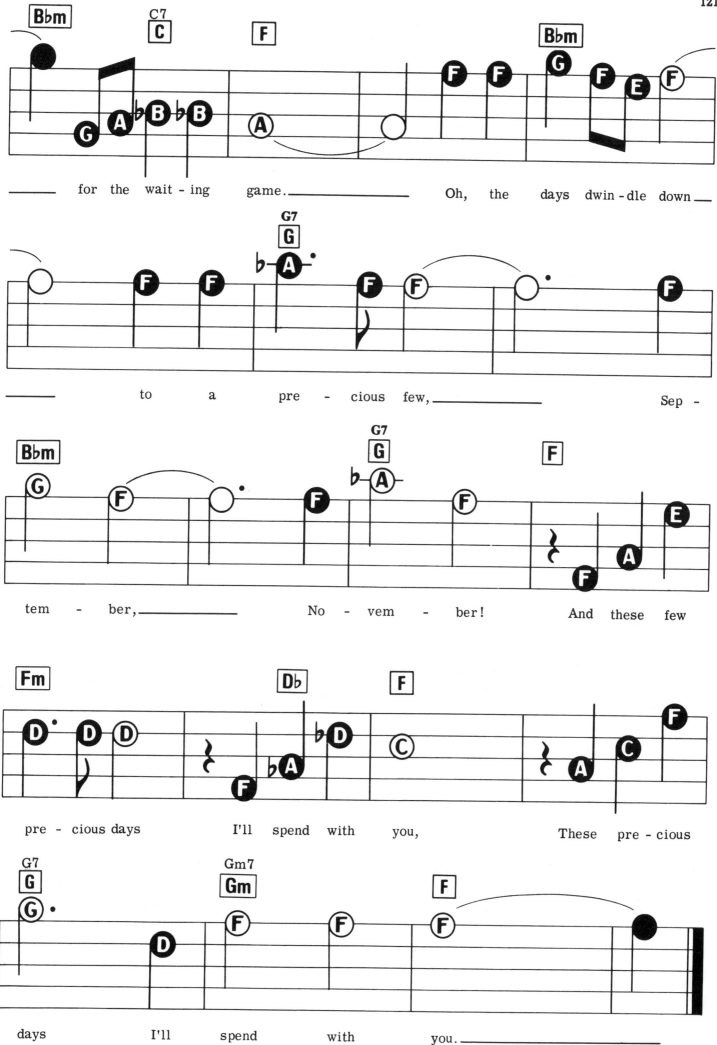

Something

Registration 4
Rhythm: Rock

Words and Music by
George Harrison

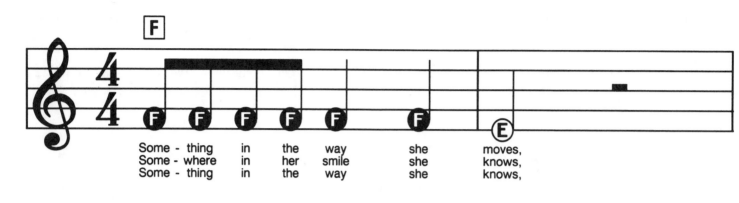

Some - thing in the way she moves,
Some - where in her smile she knows,
Some - thing in the way she knows,

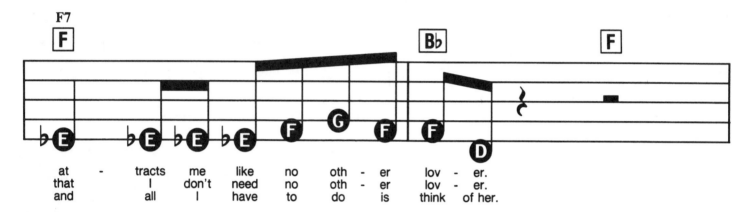

at - tracts me like no oth - er lov - er.
that I don't need no oth - er lov - er.
and all I have to do is think of her.

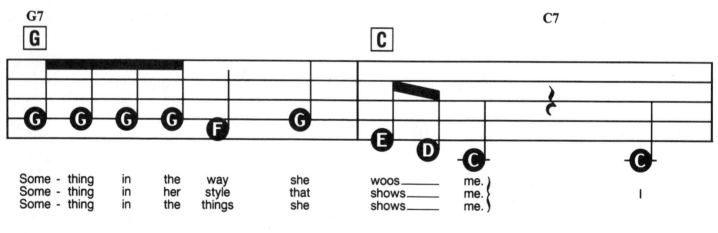

Some - thing in the way she woos_____ me.
Some - thing in her style that shows_____ me.
Some - thing in the things she shows_____ me.

I

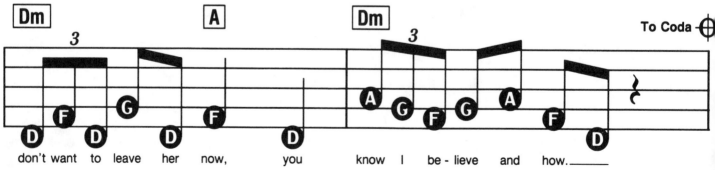

don't want to leave her now, you know I be - lieve and how._____

To Coda ✛

123

Sometimes When We Touch

Registration 8
Rhythm: Rock or Slow Rock

Words by Dan Hill
Music by Barry Mann

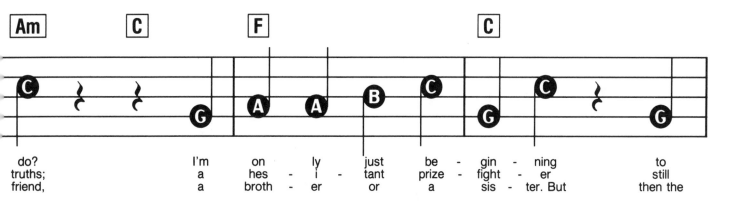

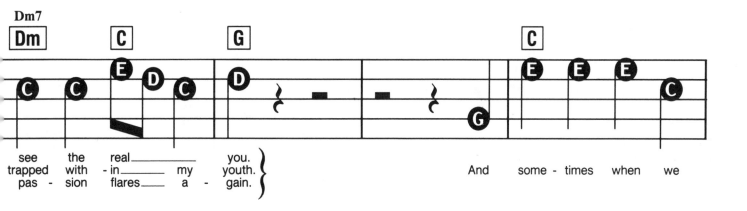

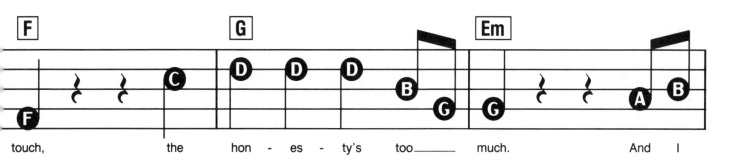

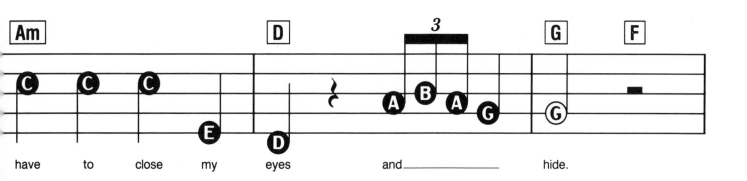

125

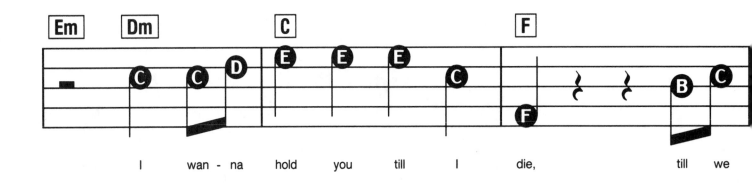

I wan - na hold you till I die, till we

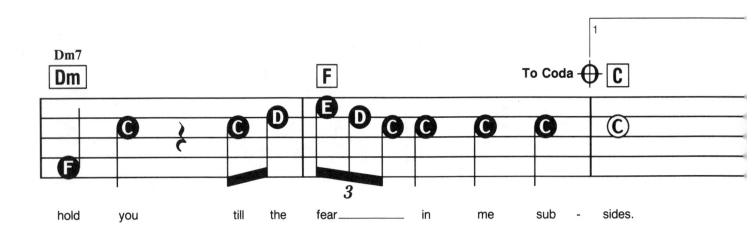

both break down___ and cry.___ I wan - na

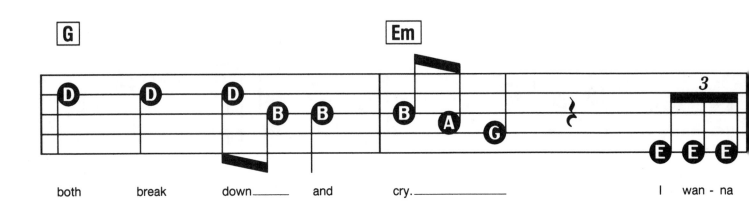

hold you till the fear___ in me sub - sides.

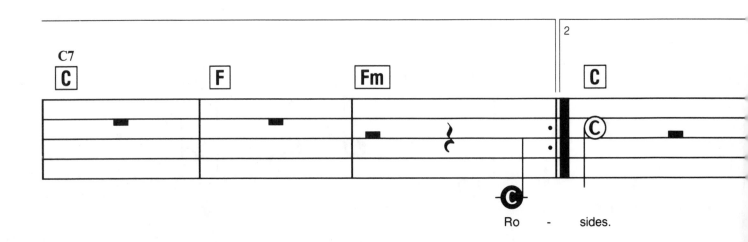

Ro - sides.

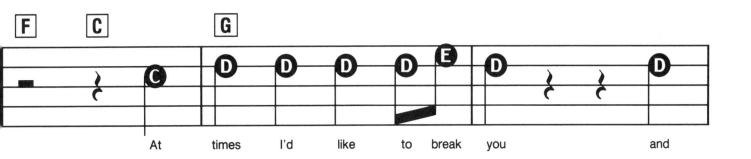

F   C   G

At times I'd like to break you and

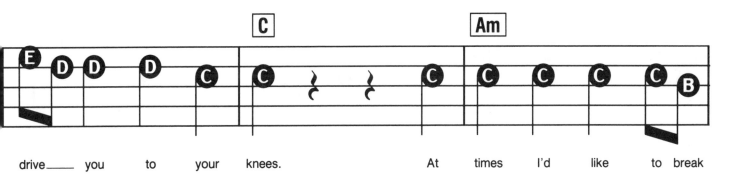

C   Am

drive____ you to your knees. At times I'd like to break

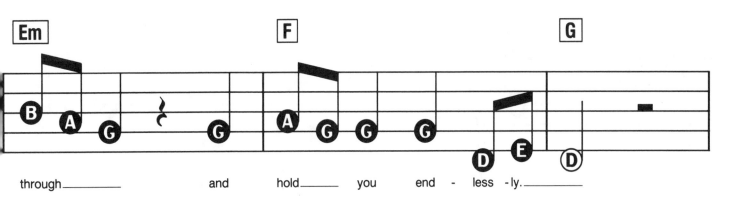

Em   F   G

through_____ and hold____ you end - less -ly.____

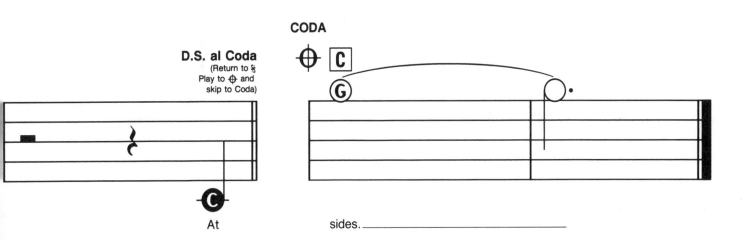

D.S. al Coda
(Return to %
Play to ⊕ and
skip to Coda)

At

CODA

C

G

sides._____

Star Dust

Registration 5
Rhythm: Swing or Jazz

Words by Mitchell Parish
Music by Hoagy Carmichael

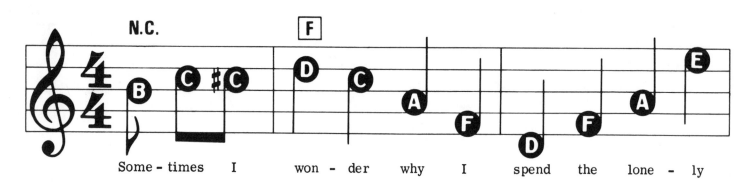

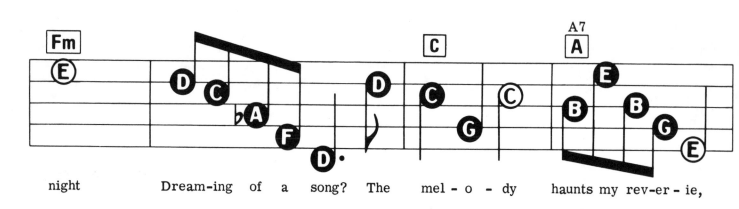

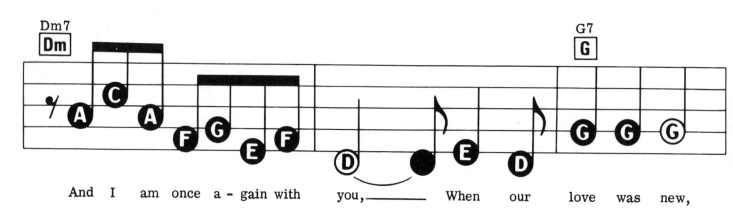

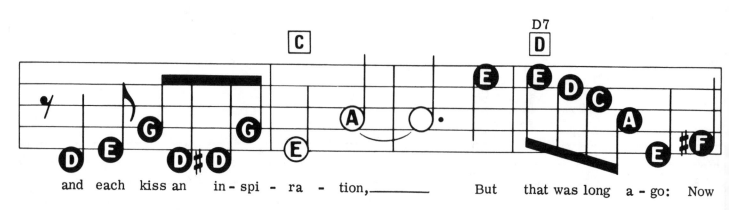

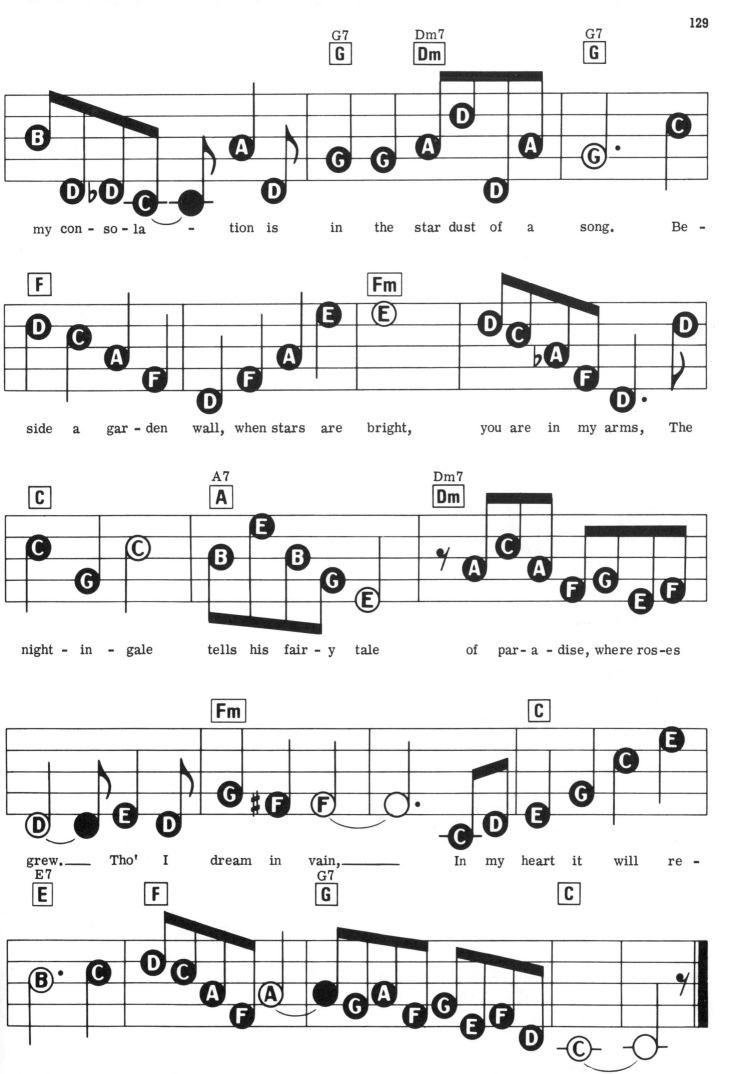

There's a Small Hotel
from ON YOUR TOES

Words by Lorenz Ha[rt]
Music by Richard Rodger[s]

Registration 9
Rhythm: Swing

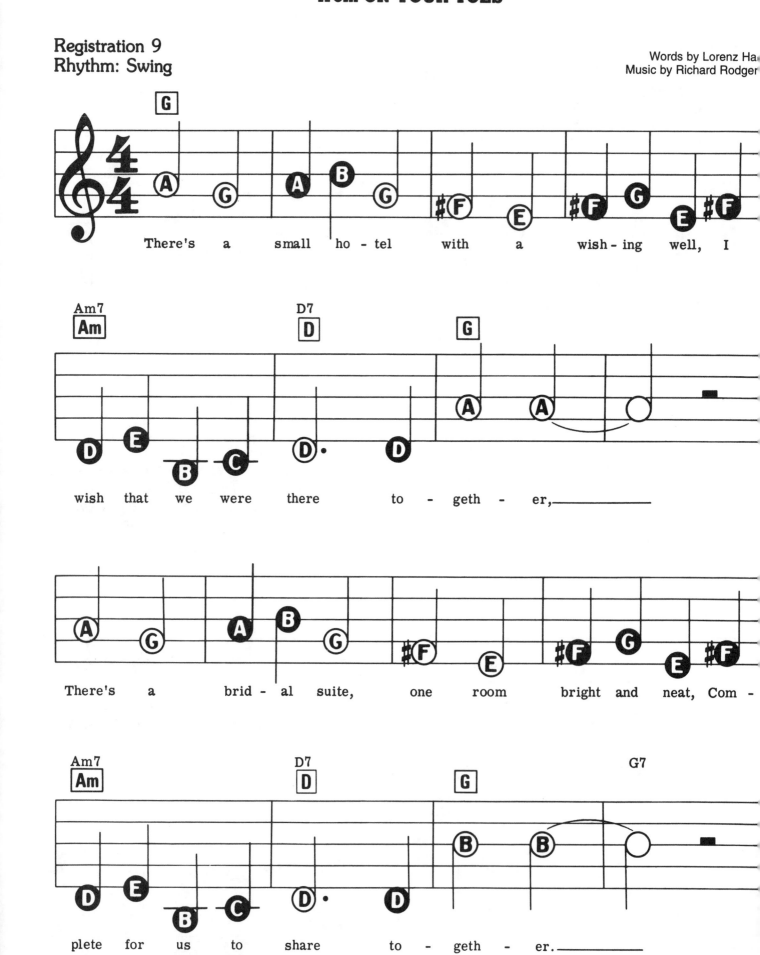

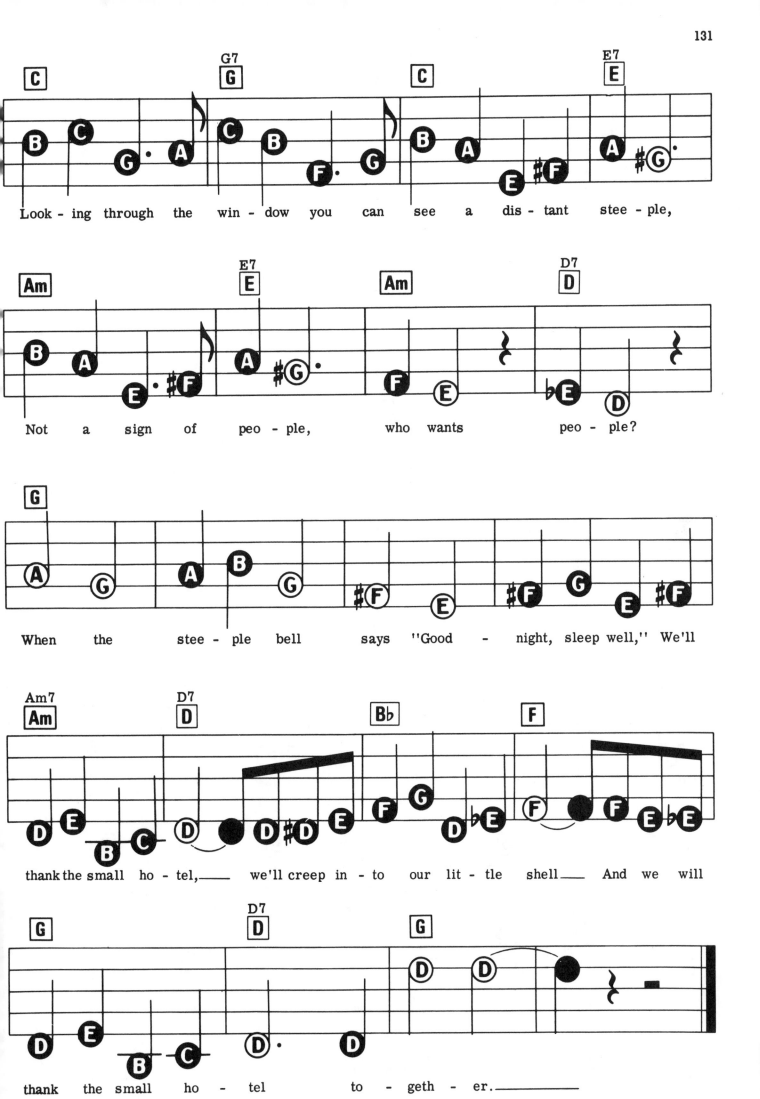

True Love
from HIGH SOCIETY

Registration 4
Rhythm: Waltz

Words and Music by
Cole Porter

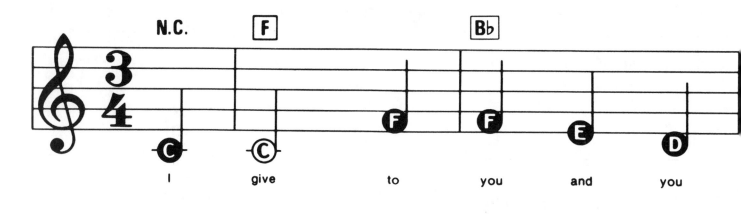

N.C. · F · Bb

I give to you and you

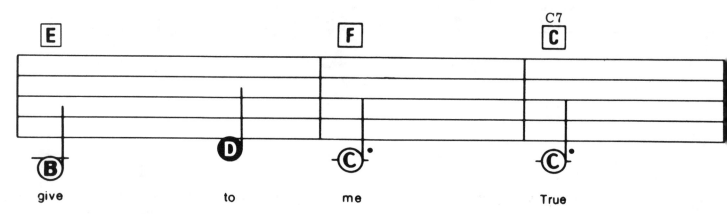

E · F · C7 / C

give to me True

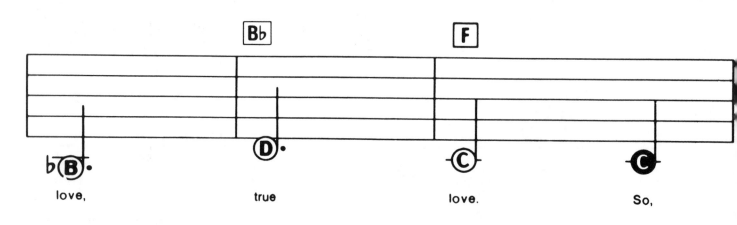

Bb · F

love, true love. So,

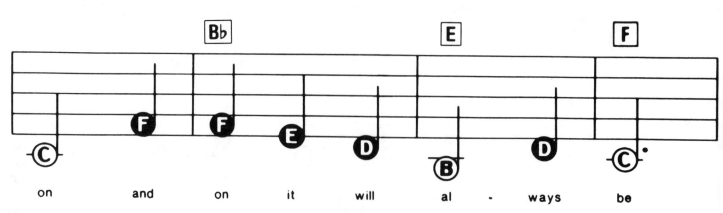

Bb · E · F

on and on it will al - ways be

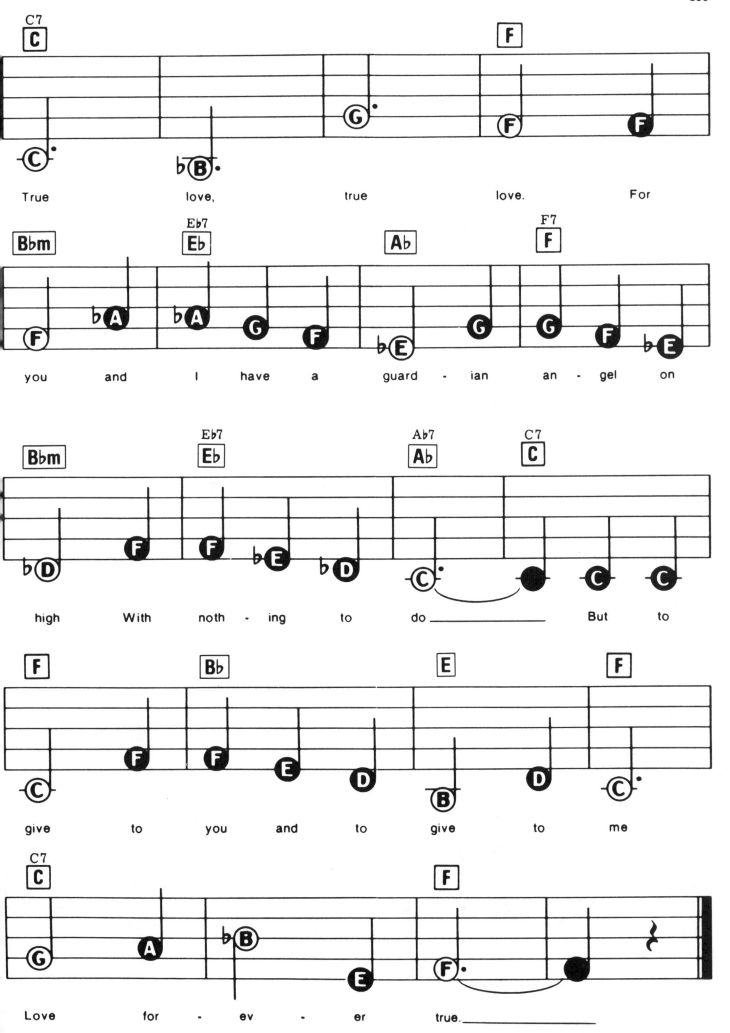

Unexpected Song
from SONG AND DANCE

Registration 1
Rhythm: Rock or 8 Beat

Music by Andrew Lloyd Webber
Lyrics by Don Black

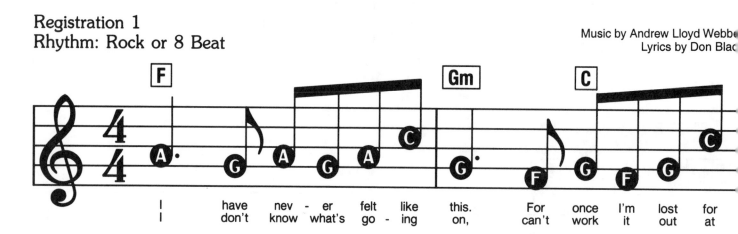

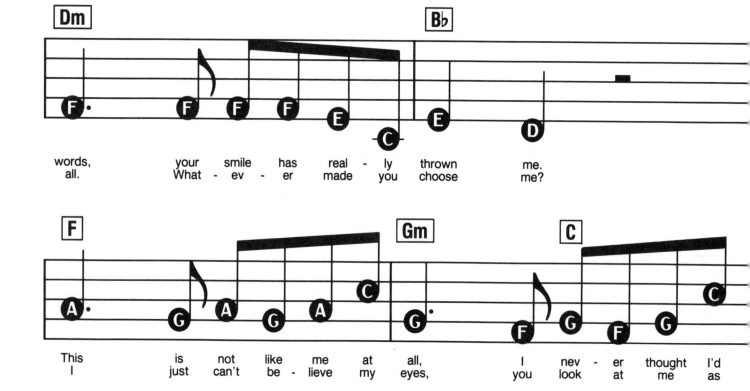

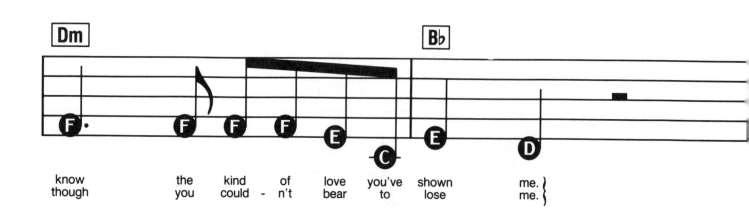

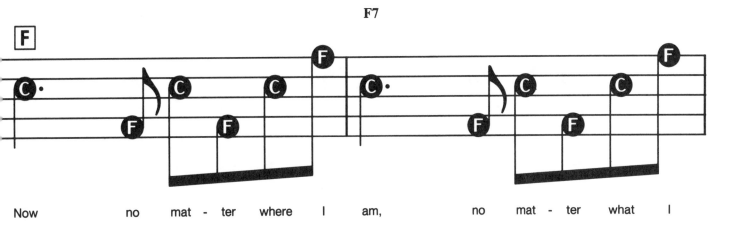

Now   no mat - ter where I am,   no mat - ter what I

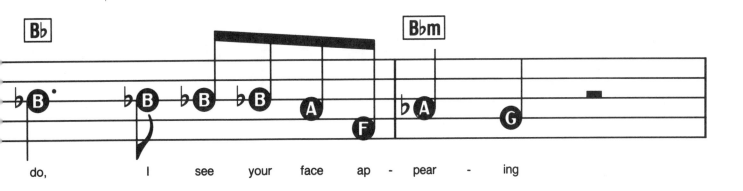

do,   I see your face ap - pear - ing

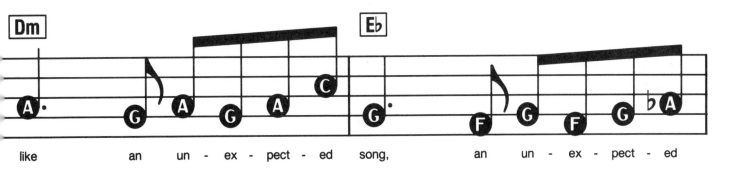

like   an un - ex - pect - ed song,   an un - ex - pect - ed

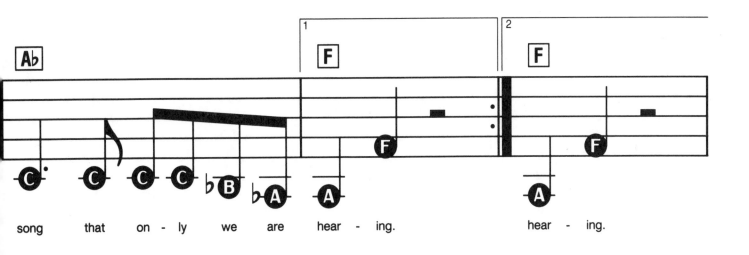

song that on - ly we are hear - ing.   hear - ing.

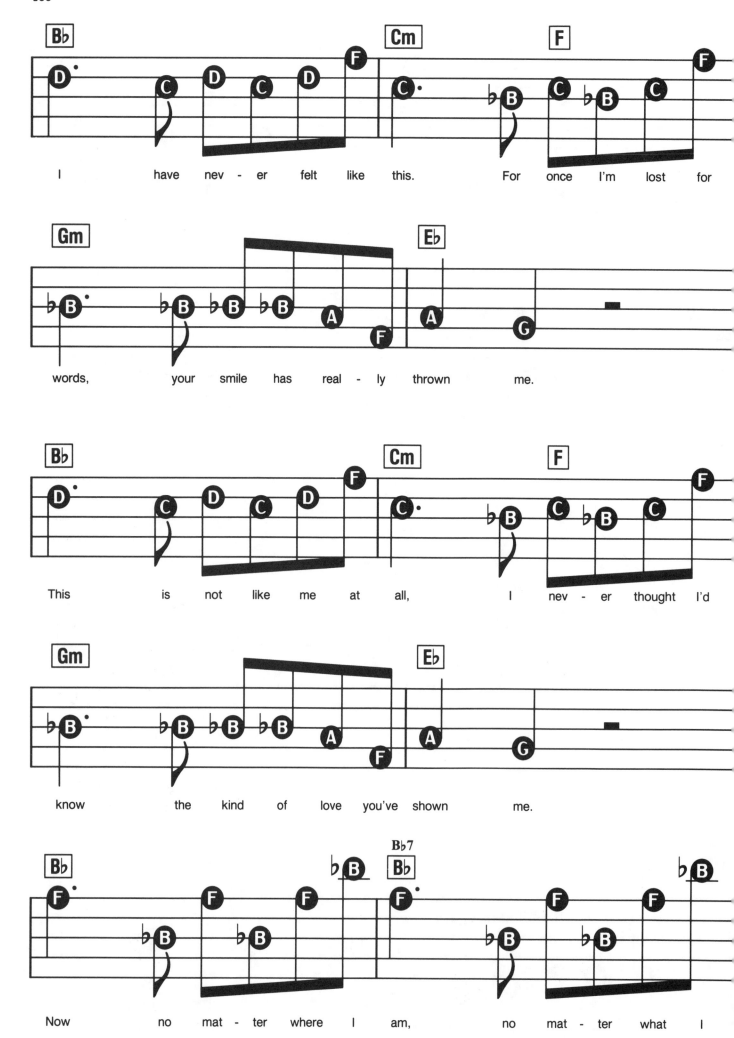

The Very Thought of You

Registration 8
Rhythm: Fox Trot or Swing

Words and Music by
Ray Noble

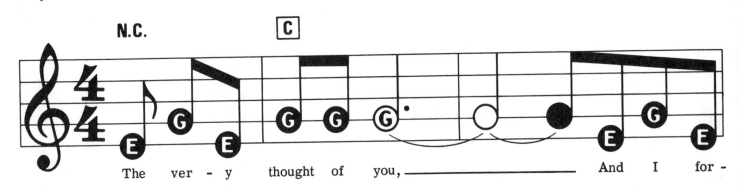

The ver - y thought of you, _____ And I for -

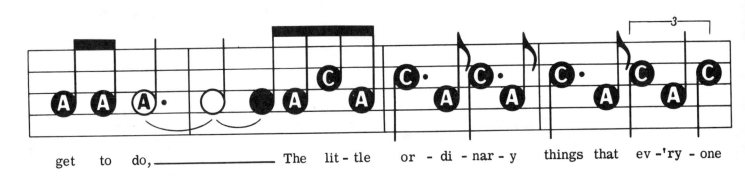

get to do, _____ The lit - tle or - di - nar - y things that ev - 'ry - one

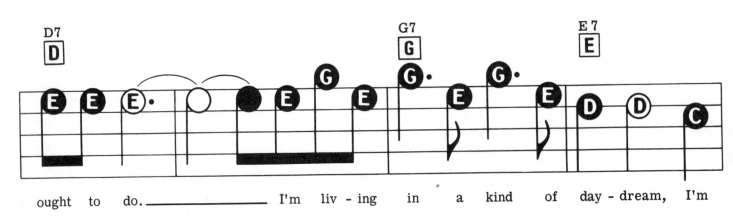

ought to do. _____ I'm liv - ing in a kind of day - dream, I'm

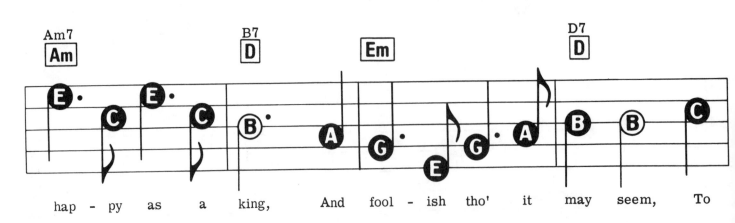

hap - py as a king, And fool - ish tho' it may seem, To

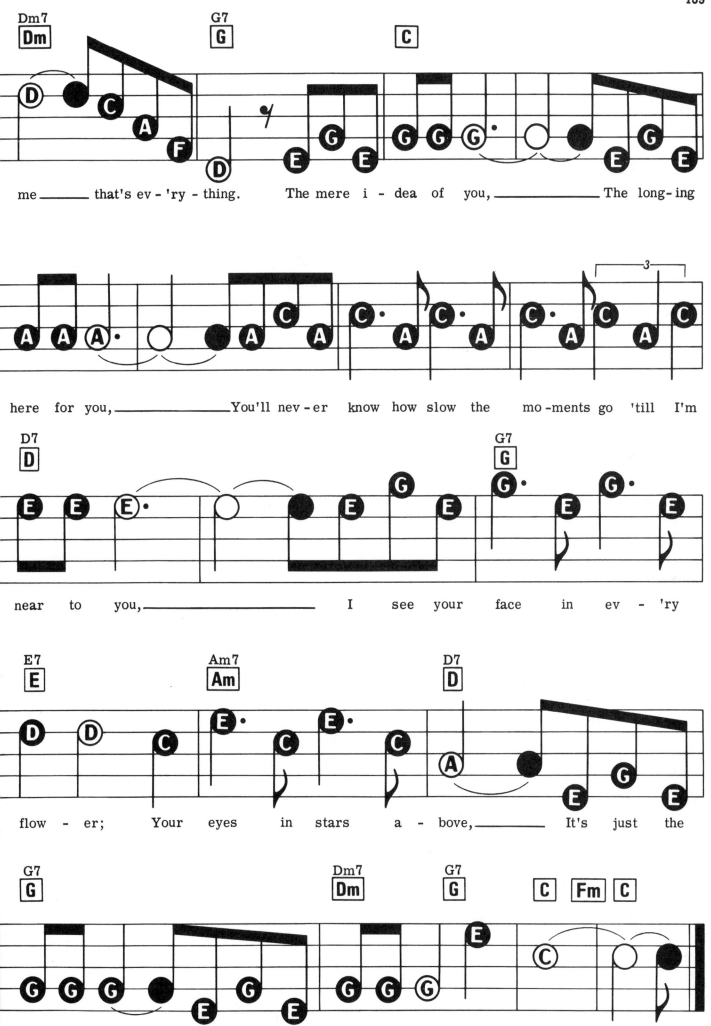

What'll I Do?
from MUSIC BOX REVUE OF 1924

Registration 2
Rhythm: Waltz

Words and Music by
Irving Berlin

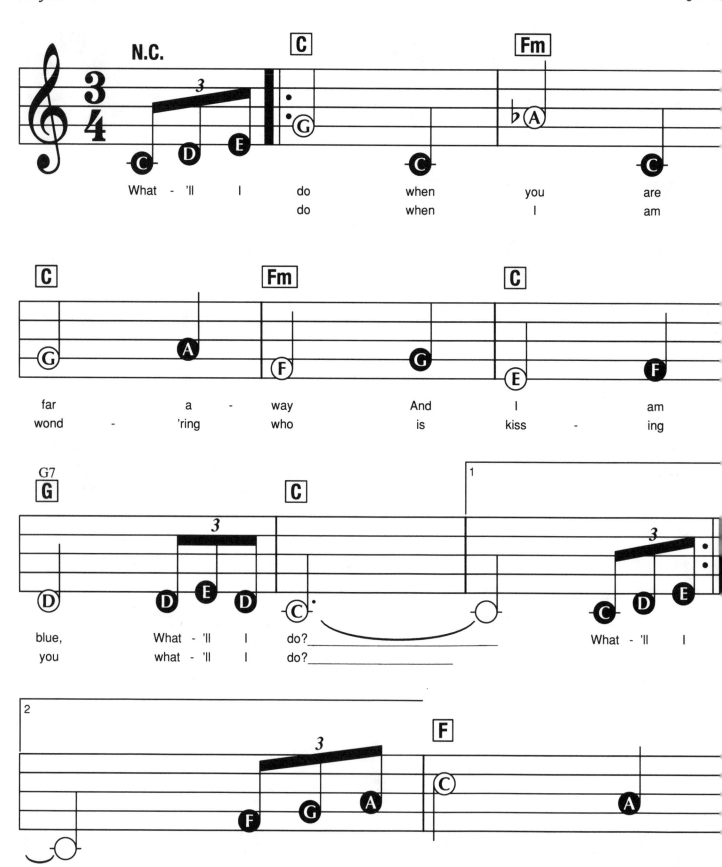

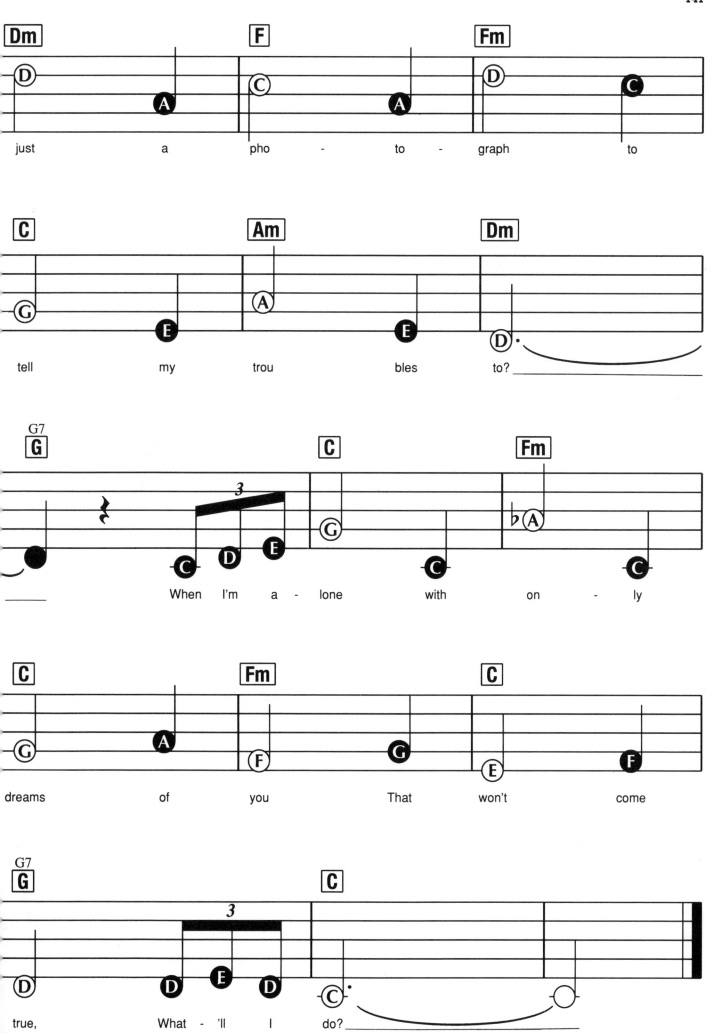

When I Fall in Love
featured in the TriStar Motion Picture SLEEPLESS IN SEATTLE

Registration 10
Rhythm: Fox Trot or Ballad

Words by Edward Heyma
Music by Victor Your

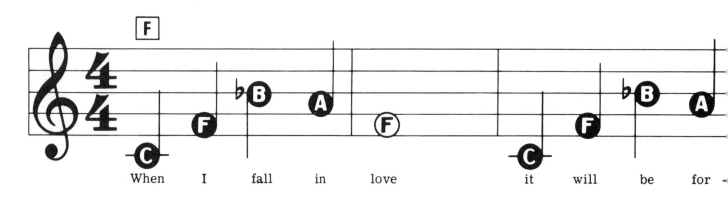

When I fall in love it will be for -

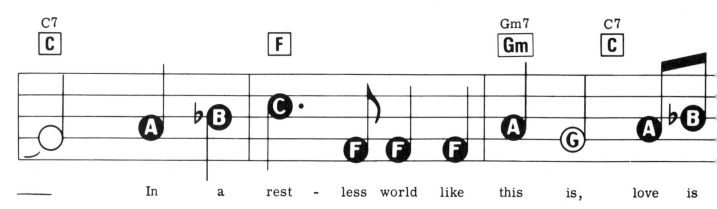

ev - er, Or I'll nev - er fall in love.

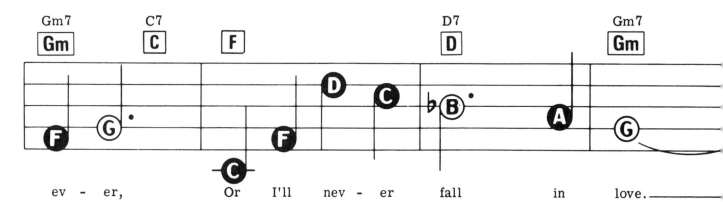

In a rest - less world like this is, love is

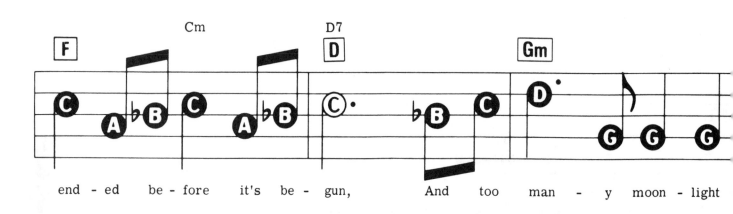

end - ed be - fore it's be - gun, And too man - y moon - light

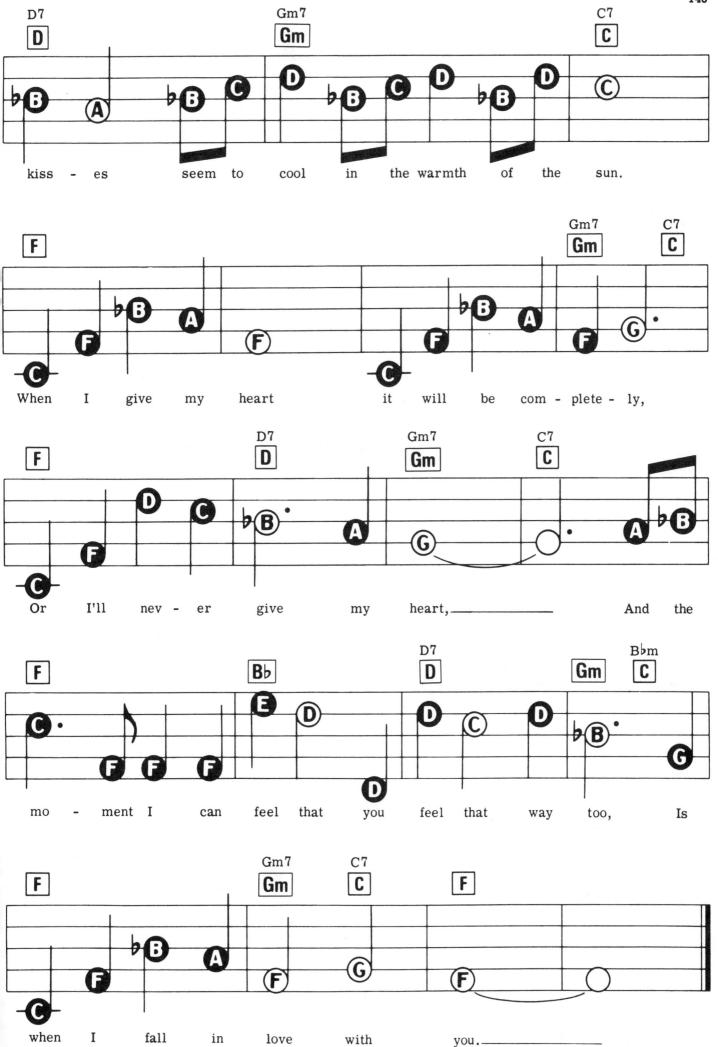

143

Where or When
from BABES IN ARMS

Registration 9
Rhythm: Ballad

Words by Lorenz Hart
Music by Richard Rodgers

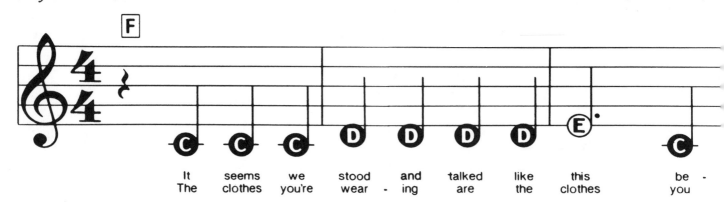

It seems we stood and talked like this be -
The clothes you're wear - ing are the clothes you

fore. We looked at each oth - er in the same way then,
wore. The smile you are smil - ing you were smil - ing then,

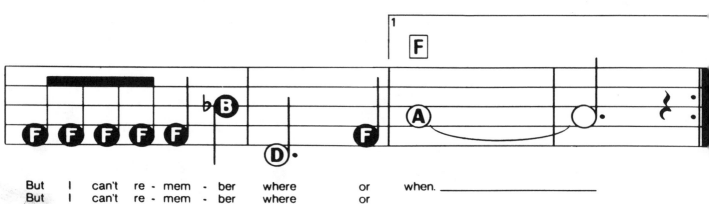

But I can't re - mem - ber where or when. _____
But I can't re - mem - ber where or

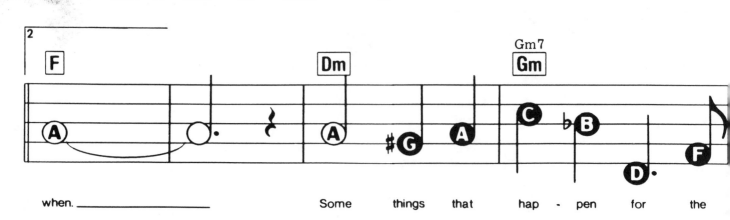

when. _____ Some things that hap - pen for the

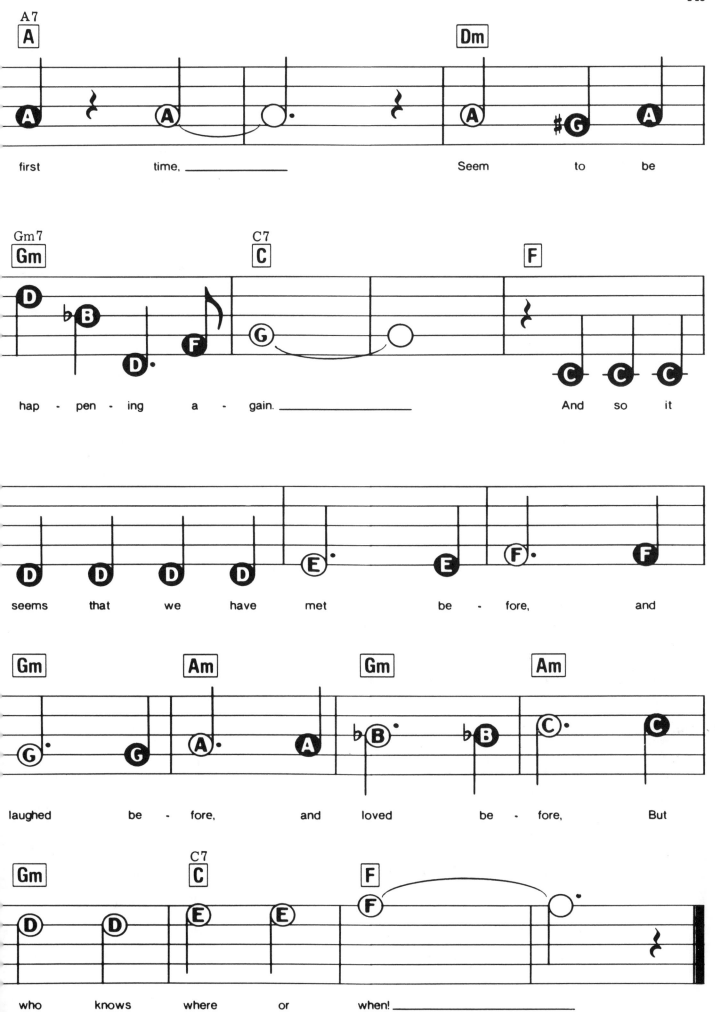

With a Song in My Heart

from SPRING IS HERE

Registration 5
Rhythm: Slow Rock or Ballad

Words by Lorenz Ha
Music by Richard Rodge

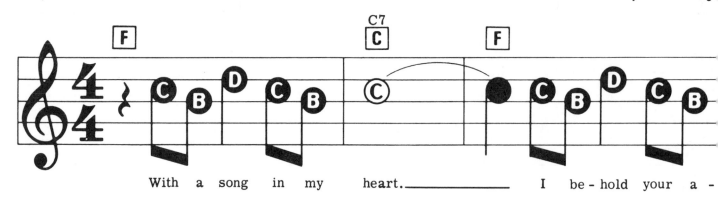

With a song in my heart._____ I be-hold your a-

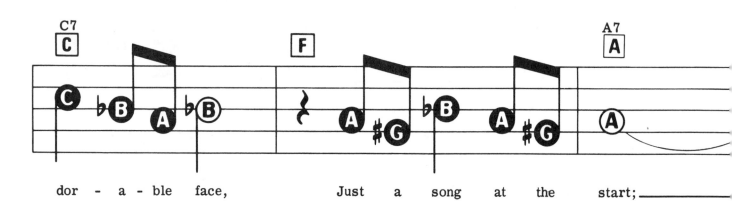

dor - a - ble face, Just a song at the start;_____

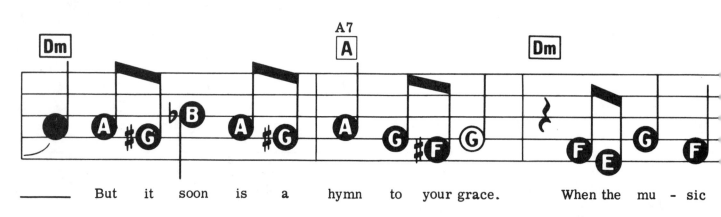

_____ But it soon is a hymn to your grace. When the mu - sic

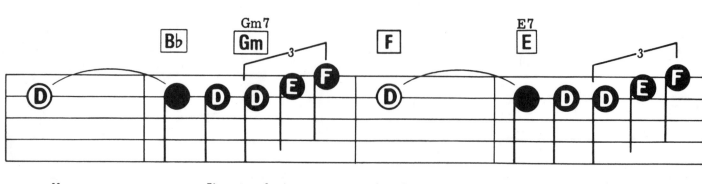

swells_____ I'm touch-ing your hand;_____ It tells that you're

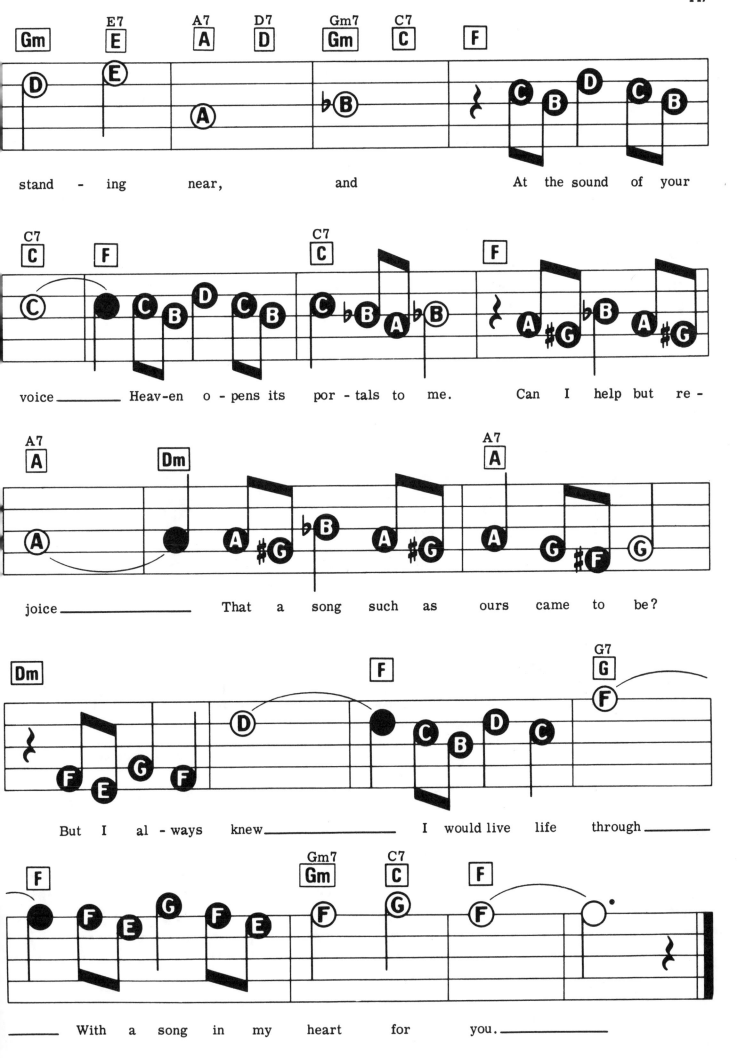

Wonderful Tonight

Registration 4
Rhythm: Pops or Rock

Words and Music
Eric Clapton

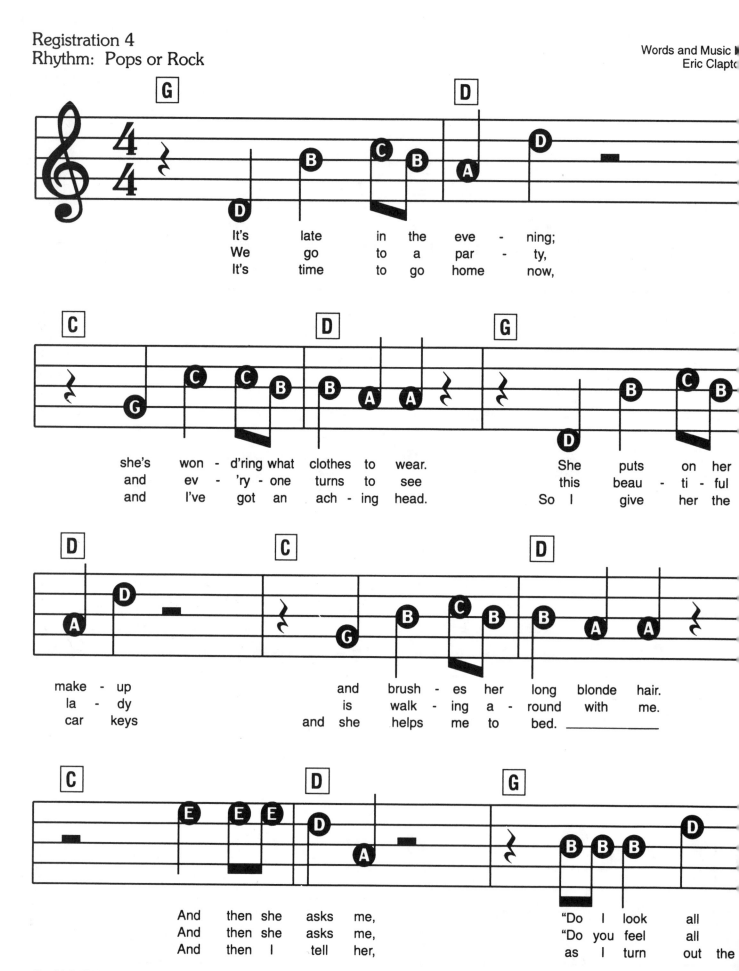

It's late in the eve - ning;
We go to a par - ty,
It's time to go home now,

she's won - d'ring what clothes to wear.
and ev - 'ry - one turns to see
and I've got an ach - ing head.

She puts on her
this beau - ti - ful
So I give her the

make - up
la - dy
car keys

and brush - es her long blonde hair.
is walk - ing a - round with me.
and she helps me to bed. _____

And then she asks me,
And then she asks me,
And then I tell her,

"Do I look all
"Do you feel all
as I turn out the

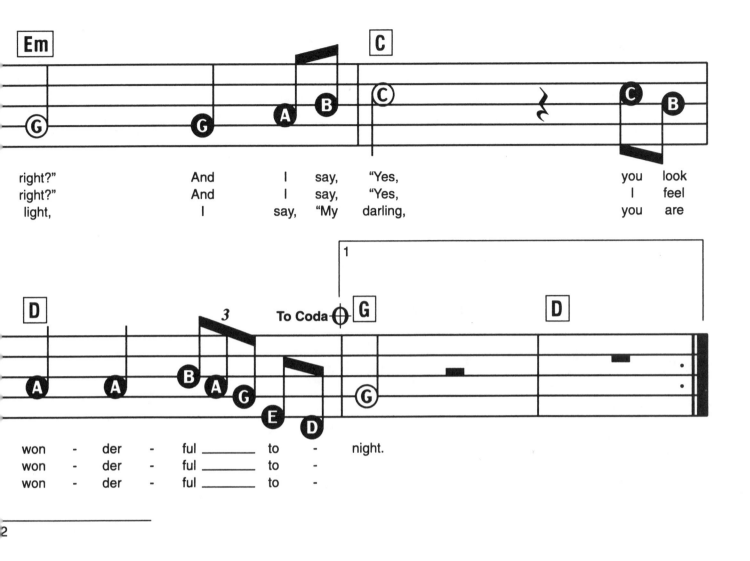

right?" And I say, "Yes, you look
right?" And I say, "Yes, I feel
light, I say, "My darling, you are

won - der - ful _____ to - night.
won - der - ful _____ to -
won - der - ful _____ to -

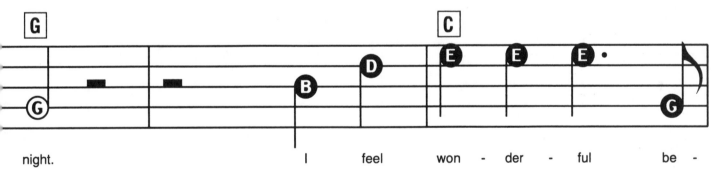

night. I feel won - der - ful be -

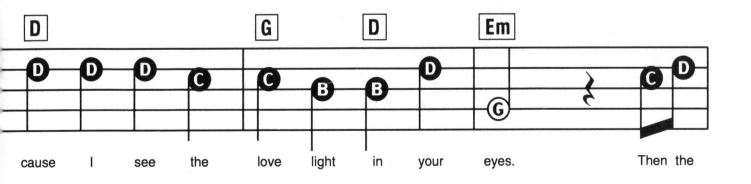

cause I see the love light in your eyes. Then the

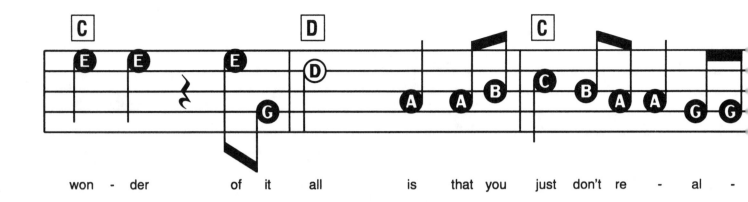

won - der of it all is that you just don't re - al -

D.C. al Coda
(Return to beginning
Play to ⊕ and
Skip to Coda

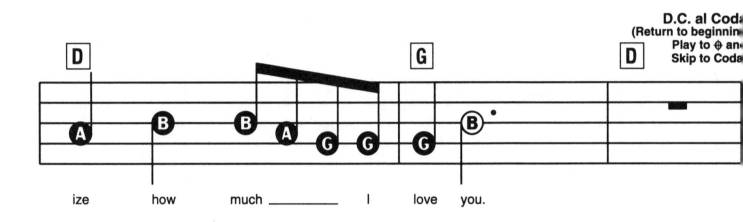

ize how much _____ I love you.

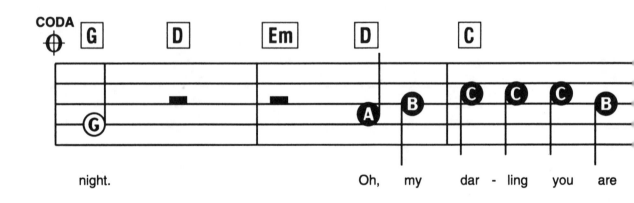

night. Oh, my dar - ling you are

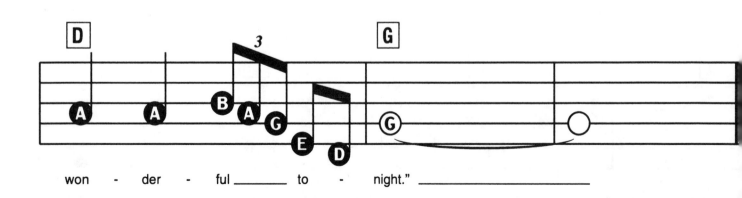

won - der - ful _____ to - night." _____

You're Nearer
from TOO MANY GIRLS

Registration 1
Rhythm: Fox Trot, 8-Beat or Pops

Words by Lorenz Hart
Music by Richard Rodgers

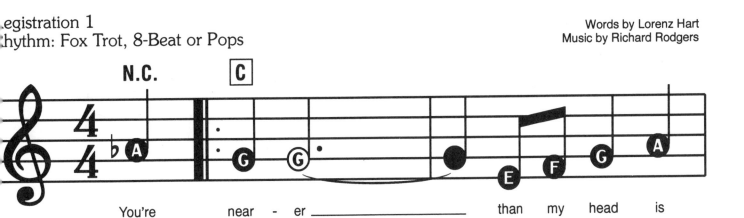

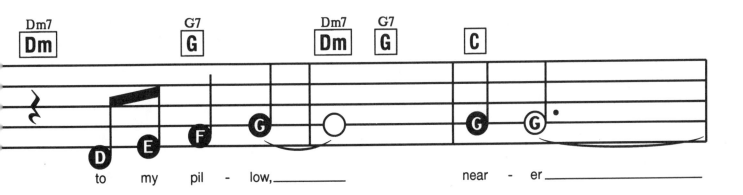

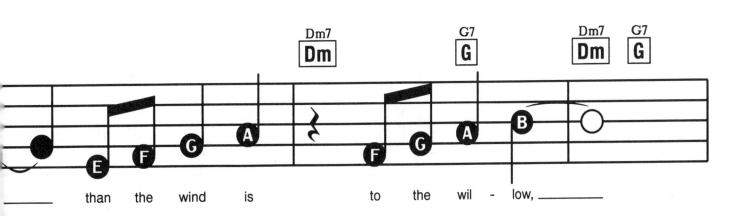

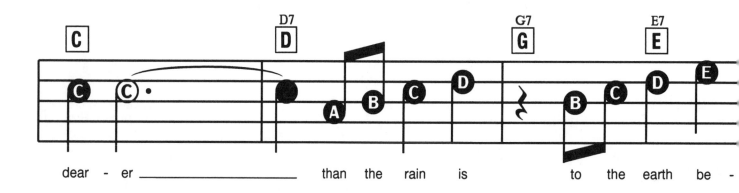

dear - er _____ than the rain is to the earth be -

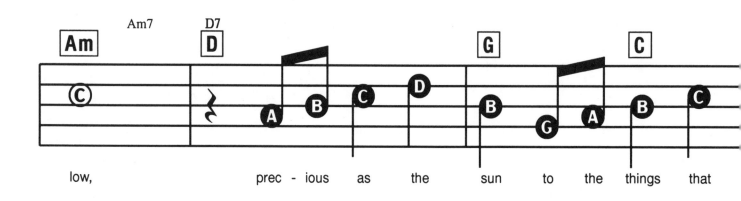

low, prec - ious as the sun to the things that

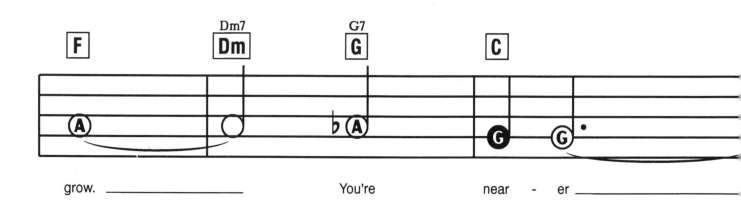

grow. _____ You're near - er _____

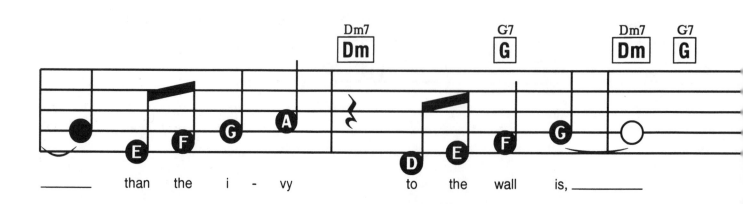

_____ than the i - vy to the wall is, _____

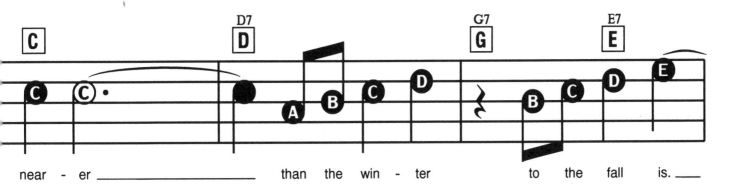

near - er _____ than the win - ter to the fall is. ____

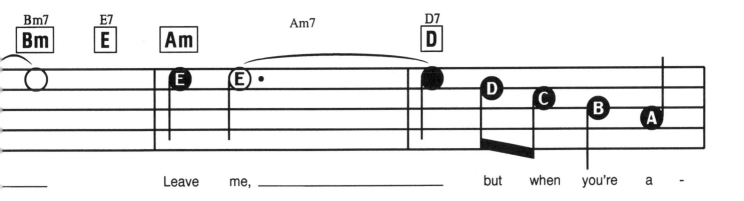

____ Leave me, _____ but when you're a -

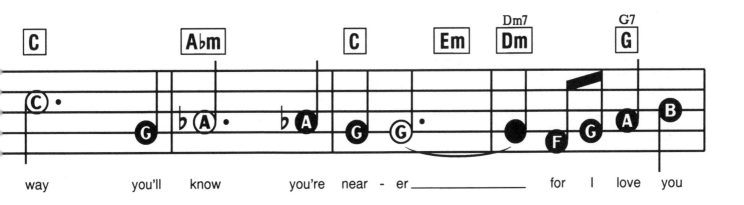

way you'll know you're near - er _____ for I love you

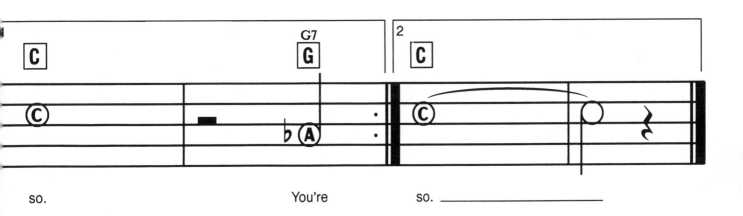

so. You're so. ____

You and I

Registration 3
Rhythm: 8 Beat or Rock

Words and Music
Stevie Wond

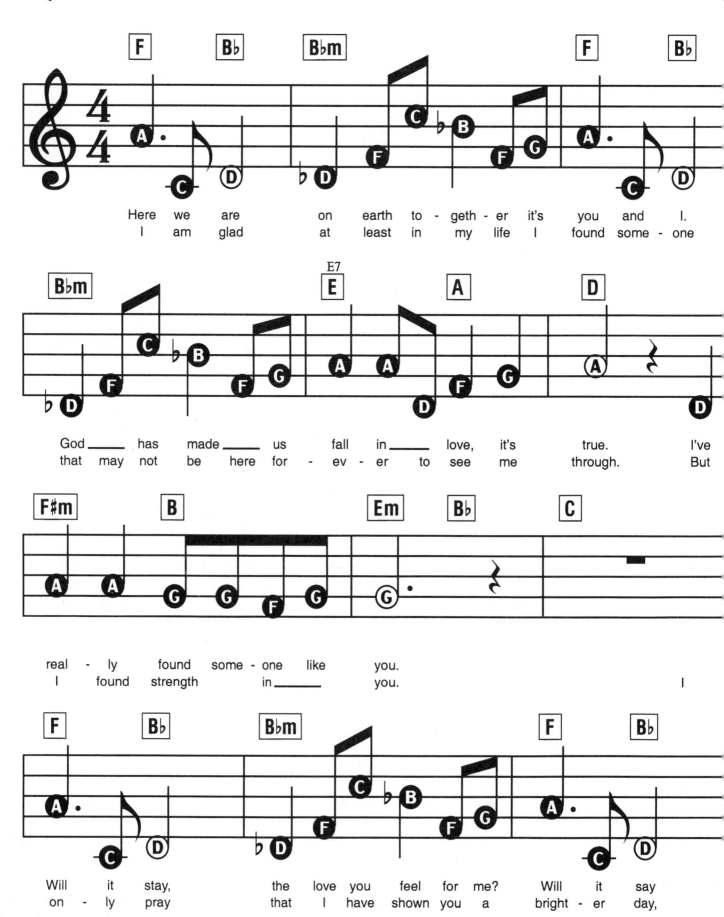

You Are the Sunshine of My Life

Registration 7
Rhythm: 8 Beat or Bossa Nova

Words and Music
Stevie Wond

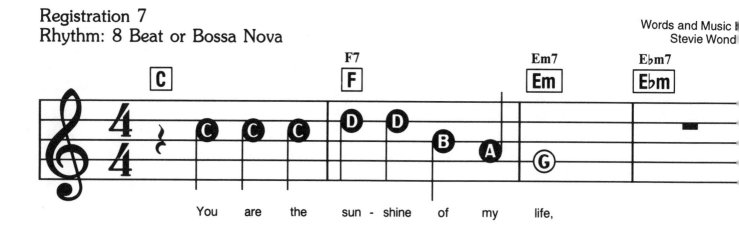

You are the sun - shine of my life,

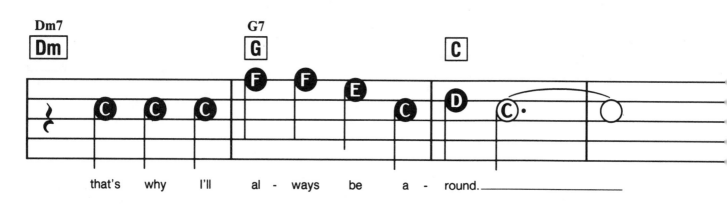

that's why I'll al - ways be a - round.

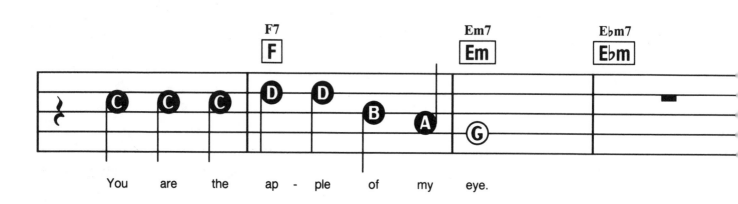

You are the ap - ple of my eye.

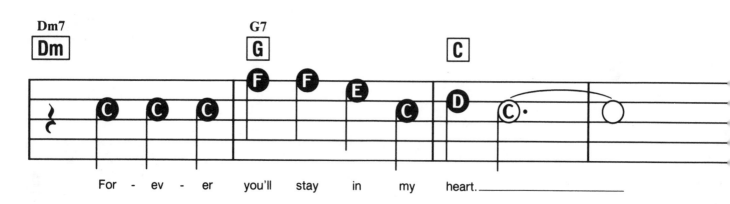

For - ev - er you'll stay in my heart.

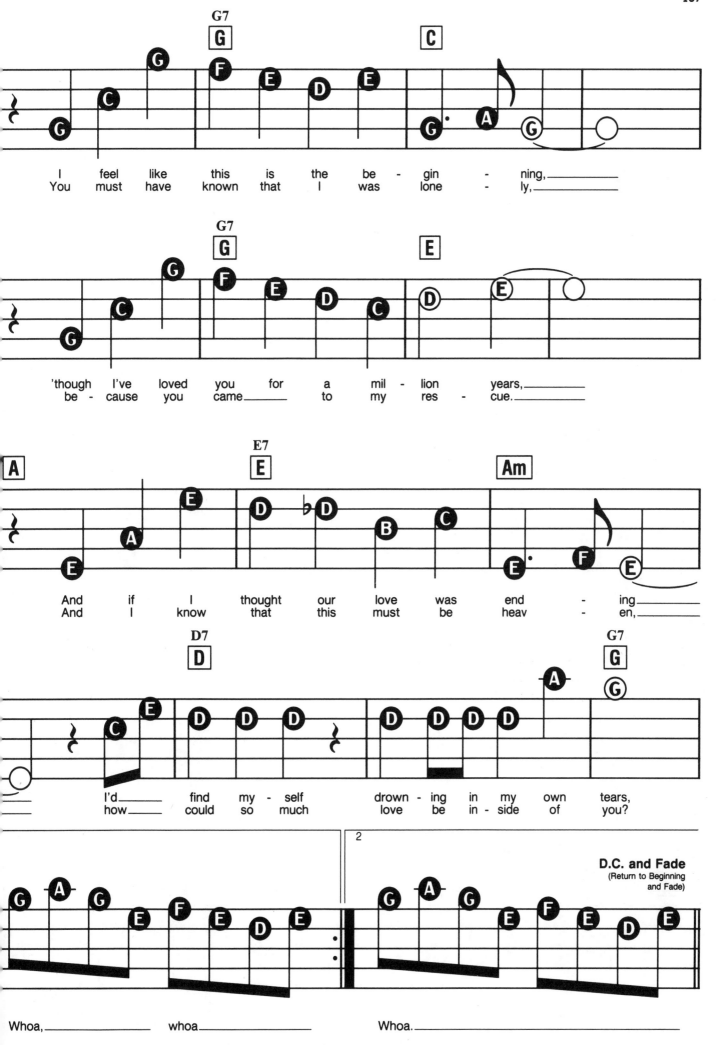

You've Got a Friend

Registration 3
Rhythm: Slow Rock or Ballad

Words and Music
Carole King

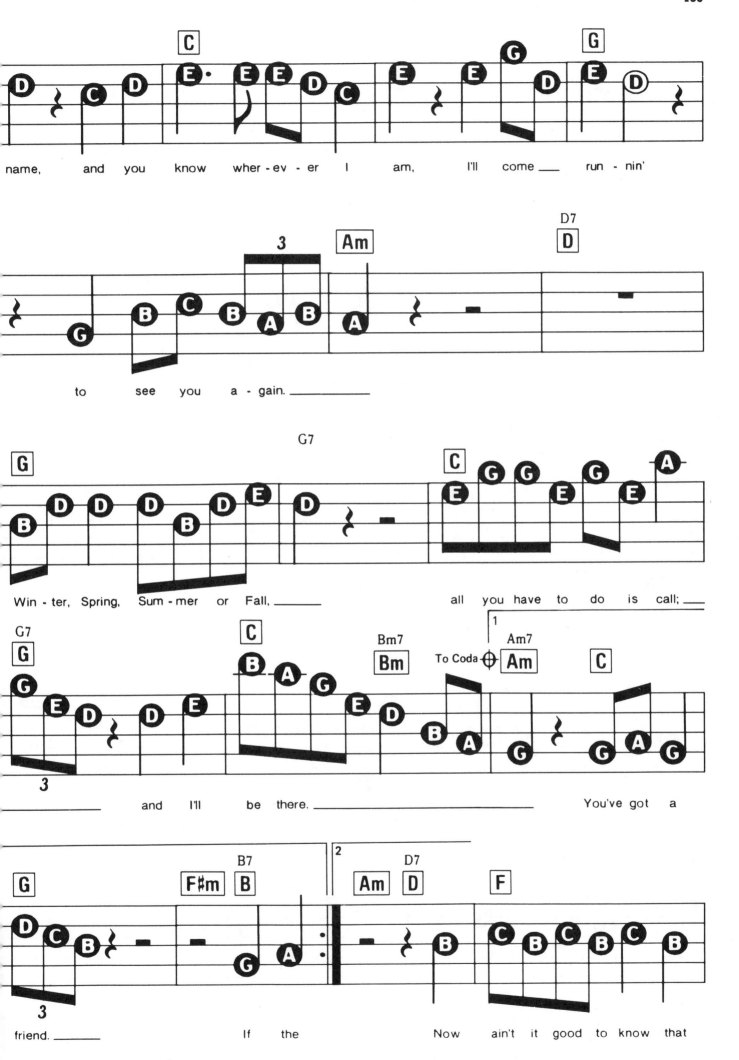

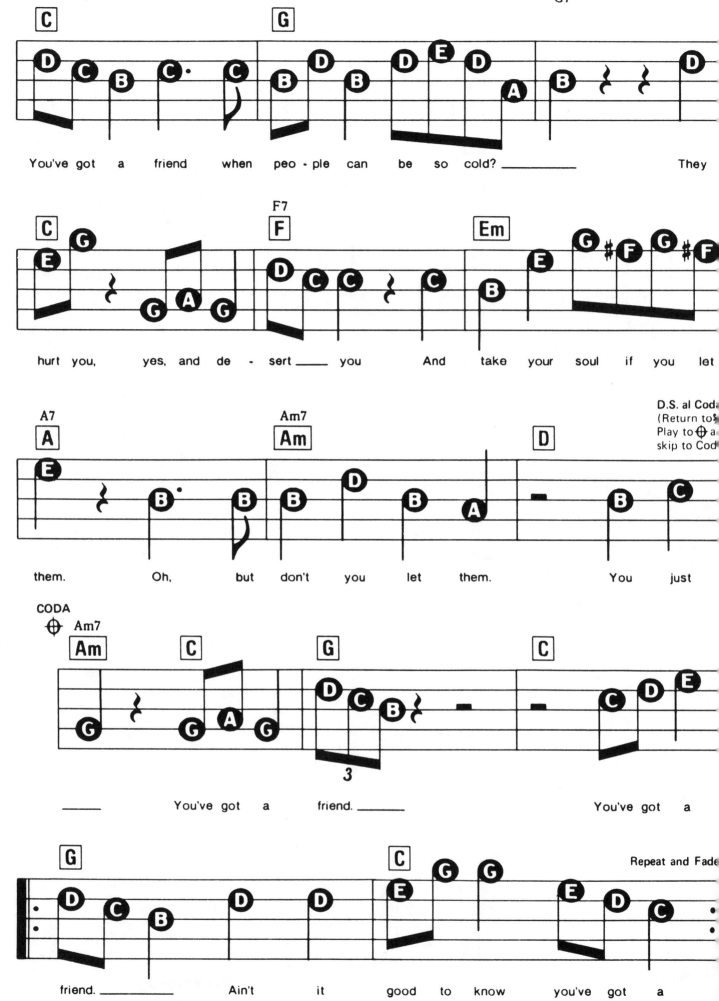